HARRY S. TRUMAN
The Man from Independence

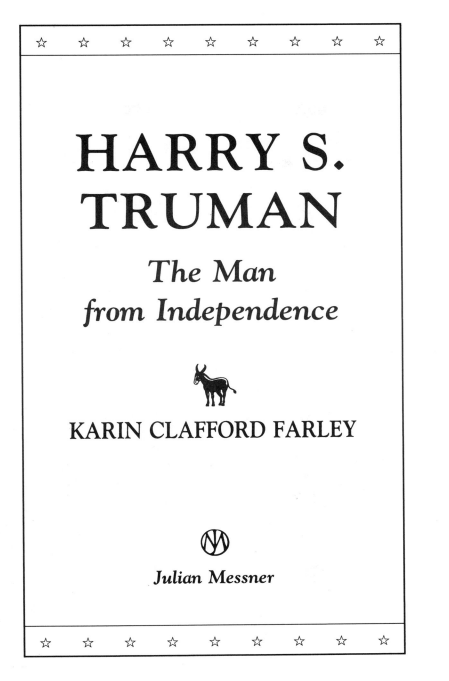

HARRY S. TRUMAN

The Man
from Independence

KARIN CLAFFORD FARLEY

Julian Messner

Published by Julian Messner, a division of
Silver Burdett Press, Inc., Simon & Schuster, Inc.,
Prentice Hall Bldg., Englewood Cliffs, NJ 07632.

JULIAN MESSNER and colophon are trademarks of
Simon & Schuster, Inc.   Design by Claire Counihan
Manufactured in the United States of America.

10 9 8 7 6 5 4 3 2 1

Quotations from Harry S. Truman, *Memoirs, Year of Decisions, Years of Trial and
Hope*, Doubleday & Co., Inc. Publishers, 1955, 1956, used by permission of Margaret
Truman Daniel.

Photographs: Harry S. Truman Library, frontispiece (Leo Stern) p. ii, pp. 4, 8, 12,
14, 19, 23, 29, 36, 37, 38, 44 (from the Kansas City Journal Post), 45 (from the
Kansas City Star), 52, 64, 65 (from U.S. Navy), 67, 73 (Abbie Rowe, from National
Park Service), 79 (from U.S. Army), 84 (from U.S. Navy), 104, 108, 110 (Abbie
Rowe, from National Park Service), 119 (from U.S. Army) 129, 131, 132. Culver
Pictures, pp. 28, 34, 56, 83. UPI/Bettman Newsphotos, pp. 53, 94, 96, 106.

Library of Congress Cataloging-in-Publication Data

Farley, Karin Clafford.
Harry S. Truman: the man from Independence / Karin Farley.
p.   cm.
Bibliography: p.
Includes index.
Summary: A biography of the only president to be born in Missouri,
a man who always kept in touch with his Midwestern roots which gave
him a common-sense approach to life.
1. Truman, Harry S., 1884–1972—Juvenile literature.
2. Presidents—United States—Biography—Juvenile literature.
3. United States—Politics and government—1945–1953—Juvenile
literature.   [1. Truman, Harry S., 1884–1972. 2. Presidents.]
I. Title.
E814.F37   1989
973.918′092′4—dc19
[B]   88–31188
                                                                         CIP
                                                                         AC

ISBN 0–671–65853–0

To my parents—
Floyd and Margaret Clafford

☆

Acknowledgments

In writing this book, I had the delightful experience of working at the Harry S. Truman Library in Independence, Missouri. It is a beautiful building and a rich source of information. The staff are truly knowledgeable, enormously helpful, and they are some of the nicest people I have ever met. They were great myth debunkers and pointed me toward the path of fact instead of perpetuating some fictions. My thanks to Benedict K. Zobrist, the director, and Philip D. Lagerquist, chief archivist, for smoothing my way and their offers of assistance. My deep appreciation to Elizabeth Safly, research librarian, and Erwin J. Mueller, who gave me all kinds of original papers and information to work with. I am especially grateful to Pauline Testerman, photo librarian, who patiently led me through many of the 84,000 pictures on file at the Truman Library while I selected some for use in this book. I also wish to thank Margaret Truman Daniel for permission to quote several passages from *Memoirs: Year of Decisions* and *Memoirs: Years of Trial and Hope* by Harry S. Truman.

To my husband, Jack Farley, for taking photos, drawing maps, proofreading, and all round support.

I am obliged to Richard G. Gallin, who edited the

manuscript with great care and interest. It has been a personally rewarding experience to research and write this book, and I am indebted to Jane Steltenpohl, Editorial Director of Julian Messner, who suggested the book to me.

Contents

Introduction

Harry Truman used to say there were three famous men from Missouri: Mark Twain, the writer; Jesse James, the outlaw; and Harry S. Truman, the only President of the United States from Missouri. Truman was born at Lamar, Missouri, in a small white house at four o'clock on Sunday afternoon, May 8, 1884. His parents, John Anderson Truman and Martha Ellen Young Truman, named him Harry after his uncle, Harrison Young. For his middle name, they wanted to honor his grandfathers, but which grandfather—Anderson Shippe Truman or Solomon Young? John and Martha decided to call their son Harry S. and let the S stand for both grandfathers' names.

After living in Harrisonville and Grandview for his first six years, Harry Truman grew up in the town of Independence. He did not leave the state of Missouri for more than a few weeks until he was thirty-three years old, when he went to fight in France during World War I. When he served in Washington, D.C. as a United States senator, then as vice president and President, he came back to Independence as often as he could. He renewed his strength by touching the ground of Missouri. The land he had farmed and his numerous relatives, long-time friends, and neighbors helped him keep his typically midwestern commonsense approach to life.

On the very day his presidency was over, Truman boarded a train for Missouri, happily looking forward to living out his life there. He died in Research Hospital in Kansas City, December 26, 1972, at the age of eighty-eight. His final resting place is beneath the soil of Missouri at the Harry S. Truman Library in his beloved Independence.

Harry Truman never pretended to be anything other than a man from Missouri, and that is what history says made him a great man.

Chapter 1

"Four Eyes"

It was almost dark. A dozen children waited in high spirits for their grandfather to use his torch to set off the fireworks. This was the best part of the Young family's Fourth of July celebration at Blue Ridge Farm in Grandview, Missouri.

With a swoosh, the first rocket shot high into the hot night sky. The children cheered as it burst into a shower of stars. Five-year-old Harry Truman and his three-year-old brother, John Vivian, stared open-mouthed at this astonishing sight. Gleefully, Vivian watched the sputtering sparks as they fell to earth, but Harry seemed to pay no attention to them. Fireworks were costly. Only a few men like the well-to-do Solomon Young could indulge his grandchildren in such delights. Each rocket, pinwheel, and Roman candle was a treat to be enjoyed to the last spark. Mrs. Truman leaned over to her son as the dying embers fell and pointed them out to him.

The skinny, brown-haired boy with the very white skin looked up at her. "I don't see any stars falling, Mamma."

Fear must have gripped Martha Truman's heart. She had noticed that when she pointed out cows or horses to little Harry he took no notice of them if they were at a distance. Now he could not see the sparks from the rockets falling

John and Martha Young Truman, parents of Harry S. Truman, on their wedding day in 1881.

around him. She decided something had to be done about Harry's eyesight right away.

Although she was expecting a baby soon, a few days later Mrs. Truman placed Harry beside her in the seat of the farm wagon. She drove fifteen miles to Kansas City to consult an eye specialist, Dr. Thompson.

Harry patiently submitted to a long examination of his eyes with his usual cheerfulness. When Dr. Thompson finished, he told Mrs. Truman about his findings. Little Harry had a rare eye deformity that could best be described as eyeballs that were flat instead of normally convex.

"Will he go blind?" she asked fearfully.

The doctor assured her that Harry would not go blind, but he would never be able to see normally. Her next question was, what could be done to help him?

Dr. Thompson shook his head. The child could be fitted with thick-lensed glasses, but that was out of the question for a young boy. He might break them and cut his eyes. Besides, such glasses would be expensive.

With fire in her own eyes, Mrs. Truman insisted her son should have glasses. How could he go to school and learn without them? The doctor warned her that if Harry wore glasses he would not be able to play games, fight, do the rough things boys did.

Then Harry would do other things, Mrs. Truman decided.

In a few weeks, Harry had his glasses and a whole new world opened up to him. He could see the small print in books. He could see the stars over the endless prairie. From Grandview, he could see the Missouri River and even Kansas City for the first time.

Harry loved living on his grandparents' farm, the largest in Missouri. He had a big swing in the backyard. His special pets were a little black-and-tan dog named Tandy, a big cat named Bob, and a black Shetland pony his father had bought for him. Harry, Vivian, and their many cousins had ponds and streams for catching tadpoles or fishing. The woods, pastures, orchards, and fields of corn, oats, clover, and wheat were their playgrounds. They were part of a large, open-hearted, extended southern family, where if a person was kinfolk, no matter how distantly related, he or she was welcome any time.

Harry was a lucky little boy to have a grandfather who was a legend in the wild West. Solomon Young was a big, powerful frontiersman. Harry heard many stories from his grandfather about the thirty years he had led long trains of huge covered wagons to Utah and California over deserts and mountains through Indian territory. He took little Harry for buggy rides behind his prize high-stepping horses when they went to the Belton Fair. Harry sat proudly in the judges' box and ate striped candy and peanuts while his grandfather awarded blue ribbons to the finest horses in Jackson County. Sometimes Harry and his grandfather got into mischief— like the time they decided to cut off little Vivian's baby curls and give him a boy's haircut. His mother was furious. Harry Truman always remembered his days at the Young farm as the happiest of his life.

But all that changed the next year when Martha Truman decided her two sons and year-old daughter, Mary Jane, needed town schooling. She wanted them to have a better education than could be had at the one-room country school near Blue Ridge Farm. She persuaded her husband to move to the town of Independence.

Independence was called the Queen City of the Trails because the Santa Fe and Oregon trails started from there. Steamboats on the Missouri River had brought settlers from St. Louis and the eastern United States. Five thousand covered wagons a year started from Independence at the height of the westward movement.

By the end of 1890 when Harry and his family moved there from Grandview, twenty miles away, Independence had changed from a frontier town to a peaceful southern community. Steam trains had replaced the Conestoga wagons. Victorian houses shaded by huge trees lined the streets. It was the proud seat of Jackson County, named after President Andrew Jackson. Like Harry's grandparents, most of the six thousand residents descended from pioneer families who had come from Kentucky. Many were kin to the Trumans and Youngs.

The Trumans moved into a big white house on Chrisler Street. It had several acres of land around it with barns and other buildings for the horses, cows, and goats John Truman traded in his business. But to Harry, it was not anything like his grandfather's farm.

Here, too, were new children who called him "four eyes" and other names because he wore glasses and could not play in their games. The other children did not understand his problems because no other children wore glasses. He could not take his glasses off to play because he said he was "blind as a bat" without them. No matter how mean the kids were to him, he covered the hurt with his natural sense of humor. But it made him feel lonely to be *different*.

The one place Harry might have made more friends was in school. But he did not go to school until he was eight. He and Vivian entered first grade together at the Noland School. Harry's mother had taught him to read when he was four years old, so schoolwork was easy for him.

Harry was a hard-luck kid. He tried to be careful about his glasses. But while he was doing as simple a thing as combing his hair in front of a mirror, he fell off a chair and broke his collarbone. Soon after that, he swallowed a peach stone and it stuck in his throat. He might have died had his mother not stuck her finger down his throat and pushed the peach stone into his stomach. Once the outside cellar

Class picture of the first grade at the Noland School. Harry Truman is the first child on the left in the bottom row.

door accidentally slammed on his left foot and completely cut off the tip of the big toe. His mother held the tip in place until Dr. Tom Twyman came and glued it back on with iodoform. Amazingly, it healed.

Worse things lay ahead for Harry. In January of second grade, he and Vivian came down with the dreaded disease, diphtheria. The doctors could do little to help the children except give them doses of ipecac and whiskey. Diphtheria antitoxin was not yet available. The great dangers of diphtheria were that the throat could swell until the patient suffocated—or the heart and nervous system could be damaged. Many children died. Vivian recovered, but Harry's arms, legs, and throat were left paralyzed. For six months, his parents had to push the nine-year-old around in a baby carriage.

He was confined to the house for a long time. His parents sent away for books. They brought him more books from the Independence Public Library to help him pass the days and weeks. Except for stories like *Tom Sawyer* and *Huckleberry Finn* by Mark Twain, few books were written for children. Harry had to read books for adults. Just as when he first got glasses, books opened up new worlds to him. He discovered history and especially liked stories about long-ago battles. Biographies of all the United States presidents were his favorites. Even after he was strong again and able to be up and about, he had his nose stuck in a book whenever he could.

During his long recovery, he was in the company of his mother much of the time. He helped her by spending hours sloshing rich milk around inside the churn to make butter. He cleaned the black smoke out of the chimneys of the oil lamps. Often he took care of his little sister. Martha Truman was a graduate of the Baptist Female College in Lexington, Missouri, where she had majored in music and art. At that time, she was one of the few women to have a college education. While they worked, Mrs. Truman discussed the books Harry was reading and passed along much of her knowledge and interests to him.

Martha Truman sought to enrich the lives of all her children. She bought a secondhand upright piano and gave lessons to Harry, Vivian, and little Mary Jane. Harry was unusually gifted and soon was beyond her ability to teach him. She sent him to study with Mrs. Edwin C. White in Kansas City. He traveled twice a week on the streetcar for lessons.

His mother and his teacher thought he would become a concert pianist. Harry thought so, too, for a while. But he paid a price. The boys in school really made fun of him. When they saw Harry with his music roll on his way to his lessons, they said playing the piano was for sissies. Like Harry, these were the grandchildren of pioneers who had fought American Indians and outlaws for a stake in Missouri. They were "fightin' boys," and if a boy wasn't a fighter, he was not one of them. But their code was never to hit somebody who wore glasses, so Harry never had a fist fight while growing up. Nevertheless, he would not stop his lessons just because other boys laughed at him.

He had experiences other boys did not have. His piano teacher had once been a fellow student of Ignacy Jan Paderewski, one of the greatest pianists that ever lived. When Paderewski gave a concert in Kansas City, Mrs. White took Harry to hear him play. Later she introduced her student to the maestro backstage. Then Paderewski showed Harry how to play his own famous composition Minuet in G. It was a moment Harry never forgot.

Harry's father saw to it that his son's life was not all reading and piano playing. Sometimes Harry rode his black pony herding cattle on drives to the stockyards at Kansas City. Every day he and Vivian, nicknamed Pete, milked the cows, curried, watered, and bedded the horses. They drove the animals to pasture in the morning and brought them back at night. Neighborhood boys and girls were always around the Truman place so they could ride the horses and ponies. Harry's father made a wagon for the children; it was pulled by goats.

Harry really admired his father and longed to be like him. John Truman was a fighter who would not tolerate injustice and lies. He would defend his honor and that of his family with his fists if need be. He would fight anyone, even though he was smaller than average in size—smaller even than his wife.

When John Truman branched out into the grain speculation and real-estate businesses, he was able to afford a better house for his family. In 1896, he traded their family home on Chrisler Street for one on Waldo Street.

Harry was now the neighbor of his cousins Ethel and Nellie Noland and of Charlie Ross and Elmer Twyman, who all went to the Columbia Elementary School. A little girl named Elizabeth Virginia ("Bess") Wallace and her three brothers also lived in the new neighborhood. They all called themselves the Waldo Street Gang.

Bess Wallace sat right behind Harry in the sixth and seventh grades and throughout high school. He had known her since he was six and started Sunday school at the First Presbyterian Church. Not only was she pretty with golden curls and big blue eyes, she was a great athlete. She played an expert game of tennis; she could ride horses; she outplayed any boy in baseball; she was a fancy ice skater on the neighborhood pond. Vivian was soon on the Waldo Street baseball team, the best one in town. But Harry could not see well enough to bat, so Bess, who played third base, said he could be the umpire.

Harry got a part-time job at Jim Clinton's drugstore across from the courthouse on the square in Independence. He opened the store at 6:30 every morning, mopped floors, swept the sidewalk, washed windows, and dusted the thousands of medicine bottles. After school he changed the displays, cranked the ice-cream machine, and made sodas. He worked all day Saturdays, too, for three silver dollars a week. After a few months, his father encouraged him to quit his job and devote more time to his schoolwork.

In Independence, elementary school ended with the seventh grade and high school lasted only three years. Harry

Harry Truman when he was fifteen or sixteen years old.

was always a good student because he read so much. He had read most of the three thousand books in the Independence Public Library by the time he reached high school. Even though Harry worked hard, he was not the smartest student in school. His friend Charlie Ross was. The teachers liked Harry and that was no accident. Every time he met new people, especially a teacher or other adult, he studied them and learned how best to get along with them. He had a cheerful personality, and he was pleasant to everyone he met.

Life was not all work. When the Spanish-American War was declared in 1898, Harry and a dozen other teenage boys formed a .22 caliber rifle company they called the Independence Junior Militia. They drilled; they camped out; they fired their guns; they marched proudly in the town's Fourth of July parade. Only fourteen years of age, they prayed the war would last until they were old enough to join up. Much to their disappointment, the war lasted only four months.

Harry graduated from high school on May 30, 1901. Far more girls than boys graduated in the class of '01. Most boys had to drop out of school to go to work. But Harry, Elmer, and Charlie planned to go to college in the fall. Harry's future looked bright indeed. As a graduation present, his parents sent him on a trip to visit his Aunt Hattie's family in St. Louis and his Aunt Ida in Murphysboro, Illinois. He had a wonderful few weeks with some of his thirty-nine first cousins.

But when Harry returned, he found that his plans for the future had collapsed. His father had lost money on grain-market investments. He could no longer afford to send Harry to college.

Independence (Missouri) High School Class of 1901. Top row: second from left is Harry Truman's friend Elmer Twyman; fourth from left with glasses is Harry Truman. Bottom row: first boy on the left is Charles Ross. Second row from the bottom: last girl on the right is Bess Wallace, later Mrs. Harry Truman.

After the first shock wore off, Harry desperately tried to save his chance at a college education. He and his friend Fielding Houchens took special tutoring in history and geography to pass the exams for a free education at West Point or Annapolis. Harry liked the idea of the military from all those battles he had read about in his books. Fielding Houchens won an appointment; Harry did not. His eyesight was not good enough.

☆ *Chapter 2* ☆

Jack of All Trades

Harry and his parents were determined that he would get additional education. In the fall of 1901, Harry enrolled in the Spaulding Commercial College in Kansas City. He studied bookkeeping, shorthand, and other business skills. He commuted daily to school from Independence on the streetcar.

But his father's money problems continued to worsen. Family expenses had to be cut even more. Harry gave up his music lessons, despite pleas from his mother and his teacher. Early in 1902, he even had to quit his classes at Spaulding College. He needed a job to help his family.

Harry was hired as a timekeeper for a construction company laying track for the Atchison, Topeka, and Santa Fe Railroad outside Kansas City. Early every morning, Harry made a list of the hundred or so men working at the railroad camp near Sheffield. Then he pumped by hand a three-wheeled car called a tricycle car over five miles of railroad track to the next camp. Again he counted who was working. He got back on the tricycle car and pumped it another five miles to the third camp at Eton. In the afternoon, he did the same thing to make sure the same men were still on the job. He worked ten hours a day, six days a week for thirty-five dollars a month and board.

Board meant Harry had to eat and sleep in the primitive railroad tent camps. The railroad workers were hoboes mostly, some of the roughest men in the country. Many had been in trouble with the law. The railroad called them gandy dancers. They did a rhythmic shuffle with their feet to firm and level the gravel bed over which the wooden ties and iron rails were laid. Though he was scared of them at first, Harry found ways to get along with them, and he learned from them. He picked up every cuss word in the English language. He also began to understand the problems of truly poor people and the seamier side of life some men chose or were forced to live.

Every other Saturday night Harry was either at Pogunjo's Saloon in Independence or Schmidt's Saloon in Sheffield. He figured his time sheets and wrote paychecks out for the railroad workers. They earned eleven dollars for two weeks' work, about fifteen cents an hour. Most of them immediately spent their meager pay on liquor. Sobered up and flat broke by Monday, they showed up on the job for another two weeks' work.

Perhaps it was this education in the ways of virtueless living, or maybe it was the urging of his mother, that led eighteen-year-old Harry to join the Baptist church. He said, "I've always believed that religion is something to live by and not to talk about. I'm a Baptist because I think that sect gives the common man the shortest and most direct approach to God."

After the railroad job was finished, Harry found work in the mail room of the *Kansas City Star* newspaper. He wrapped papers for nine dollars a week and turned his salary over to his family.

John Truman was forced to sell the house on Waldo Street and buy a small house on Park Avenue in Kansas City. He sold all his property to pay his debts. He was a man of great honor and integrity. To raise money, Martha Truman disposed of a 160-acre farm her father had willed to her. With no resources left except their Kansas City house, John Truman took a job as a night watchman at the Missouri Elevator Company down on the river. Only two years before, he had been the associate of some of the richest and most powerful men in Kansas City.

Harry and Vivian applied for jobs at the National Bank of Commerce in Kansas City. It was the largest bank west of the Mississippi River. They were put to work down in the vault in the basement of the bank. The young men and boys who worked down there called it "the Commerce Zoo" because they worked in iron cages. That was bad enough, but the "zoo keeper" was a vice president of the bank in charge of hiring and firing employees like Harry and Vivian. He took great pleasure in publicly chewing out these poor employees for the slightest error in arithmetic or any infraction of the rules. Harry worked hard and tried to get along with people. But he soon realized he had little chance of wage increases or promotion at the National Bank of Commerce.

In 1904, John Truman sold their home in Kansas City for an eighty-acre farm in Clinton, Missouri. After Harry helped his parents move to Clinton, he and Vivian went to live with their father's sister Emma Colgan and their cousins. But they did not live there long because Harry was fond of practical jokes. He decided to write letters to his cousin Fred Colgan from some imaginary ladies. He even had the letters postmarked in Mississippi. When Fred found out what a fool had been made of him, he stopped speaking to Harry. So did Harry's Aunt Emma. Harry had to find another place to live.

The Truman brothers moved into a boardinghouse on Troost Avenue in Kansas City where other young bank clerks boarded. They got a room plus breakfast and dinner every day for five dollars a week. Harry became good friends with another guest, a young bank clerk from Kansas named Arthur Eisenhower. They shared an interest in music and reading.

Harry enjoyed life in Kansas City. While working at the bank, he got a job ushering on Saturday afternoons at the Grand Theater. All the best vaudeville acts in the world sooner or later appeared at the Grand. When Harry was not working, he had wonderful times going on picnics, on boat rides on the Missouri River, and to theaters and restaurants. Harry, his young cousins, and their friends loved the bright gaslights and excitement of fast-growing Kansas City.

Early in 1905, Harry quit the National Bank of Commerce and went to work at the Union National Bank, where his hard work and cooperative ways were recognized. Soon he was promoted to assistant teller and paid one hundred dollars a month. This was an excellent salary in the first years of the twentieth century.

Harry turned twenty-one years old in 1905. A full adult at last, he did something he had always wanted to do. He joined a new Missouri National Guard unit being formed in Kansas City. It was not West Point, but it was the military. Harry's friends from the bank joined, too. Once a week they

The house at Blue Ridge Farm in Grandview. Martha Truman (Harry's mother) is standing; Harriett Louisa Young (his grandmother) is sitting. Harry Truman is in his farm clothes taking a little time off from work.

paid a quarter to go to the armory to drill. Some weekends they trained out in the country. Every summer they spent two weeks at camp where Harry learned to fire an artillery gun. He was well suited to the artillery because he could handle the horses needed to pull the big guns. Though only a private, he walked tall when he wore his blue uniform with its red stripes.

On most Sundays, he visited his parents in Clinton or Grandmother Young and Uncle Harrison in Grandview. During one of these visits, Uncle Harrison proposed that John and Martha Truman move back to the Young farm. Harrison wanted to retire. Harry thought this was a good idea because the Trumans' Clinton farm had been flooded out by spring rains. But when Harry proposed it to his parents, his father hesitated. John Truman was in his fifties, and without Harrison Young, he would need Harry's help to manage the large farm. Loyalty to family and friends was the cornerstone of Harry Truman's life. His parents needed him. Much as he enjoyed his life in Kansas City, he willingly quit his job at the bank. By 1906, the Trumans were together again on the Young farm in Grandview.

Blue Ridge Farm was no longer the magnificent estate of five thousand acres it had been during Solomon Young's lifetime. It had shrunk to about nine hundred acres. Everyone always had endless work to do. Harry was no gentleman farmer or even the overseer; he was just another farmhand. He and Vivian were in the fields at five in the morning plowing, sowing, cultivating, or harvesting. Under the supervision of his father, Harry learned how to work the land with great care.

Harry was not satisfied to farm as his grandfather and father had. He sent away to the Universities of Iowa and Missouri and to the U.S. Department of Agriculture for advice on scientific farming. Rotating crops—planting clover one year followed by corn, oats, and wheat, and then starting all over again with clover—doubled and tripled yields per acre. He was the first farmer in the region to vaccinate his Hampshire hogs against the disease of cholera. He kept careful records of animal and crop production and practiced soil conservation.

Harry found time to do other things besides work on the farm. He would come in from the fields for noon dinner break, sit down at the upright piano in his grandmother's parlor, and practice Mozart and Beethoven. His rough, calloused hands glided expertly over the keys. He joined a Masonic Lodge and studied diligently to rise in that organization.

For the first few years, the farm made a good living for the Trumans. Then in 1909, Harry's grandmother, Harriet Louisa Young, died at the age of ninety-one. Her death marked the beginning of financial problems for the Trumans that would last the rest of their lives. In her will, Louisa Young left her fortune to her son Harrison and daughter Martha Truman. Her other five children and her grandchildren by them were angry at being cut out of their mother's will. They filed legal action against Harrison and Martha. In order to pay legal fees, Mrs. Truman had to heavily mortgage the farm; that is, she borrowed a large amount from banks. If she was unable to pay the money back, the banks would take over Blue Ridge Farm. All the profits from the farm from 1910 on went to the banks and the lawyers. The big dreams Harry was beginning to dream seemed to have little chance of fulfillment.

Harry was twenty-six. It appeared he would take after his uncle Harrison Young and remain a bachelor. He never really dated anyone, and when he went to parties, he escorted one of his cousins. One weekend in the summer of 1910 Harry went to visit his cousins the Nolands in Independence. This particular day, Ethel remarked that she should return a cake plate to Mrs. Wallace who lived across the street. On hearing that name again, Harry quickly volunteered to do this small service. When he rang the Wallaces' doorbell, Bess opened the door. Harry and Bess had not seen each other since they had graduated from high school nine years before. They spent two hours that evening catching up on those years.

When he left, Harry asked if he might call on her again and she agreed. He began going to Independence every weekend he could find an excuse to get away from the farm. Although they both had telephones, Harry did not trust his ten-party "pumpkin vine" where nine of his neighbors could listen in if he called Bess. Instead, they wrote letters and exchanged books between visits. Harry saved dimes to buy all the books written by Mark Twain, his "patron saint of literature." Bess tried to persuade him to read Charles Dickens.

About a year after they became reacquainted, Harry proposed marriage to Bess. Too shy to ask her in person, he wrote her a letter. The letter hardly fulfilled the romantic dreams of a young woman. Harry told her he had cared about her since they were in the church kindergarten class and asked, would she wear a diamond ring on her left hand? These two sentences were sandwiched in among discussions of rural gossip and failing crops owing to lack of rain. No wonder Bess did not answer for several weeks. When she did, her reply was that she was not ready to marry anyone.

Harry was deeply in love with her. Though she could not return his love, Bess agreed they could remain friends. For this, Harry was grateful. He had been taught by his father and Grandfather Truman always to treat women and girls with the greatest respect and courtesy. Even as children, Harry and Vivian had been charged with protecting and defending their little sister at school and at play. Anything Bess or any of the women in his family wanted was all right with Harry.

Over the next two years, Harry's unflagging devotion and attention slowly won Bess's heart. In 1913, she accepted

Young Bess Wallace sitting on the porch railing at 219 North Delaware Avenue, Independence, Missouri.

his proposal, but they kept their engagement a secret. Harry could not even afford to buy her a ring.

That same year, the United States went into an economic recession. Farm prices went down. To cut expenses, Harry dismissed all the hired hands and tried to run the farm himself. But he could not make any more money despite his backbreaking work. In 1914, his mother's legal suit with her brother and sisters was settled out of court. Martha Truman and Harrison Young still owned Blue Ridge Farm. When John Truman died that same year, Harry was burdened with his father's medical expenses and more debts.

These debts and the prospect of marriage to Bess spurred Harry to find ways to make more money. He seized upon the chance to sell real estate in Texas in addition to running the farm, but that venture did not work out.

Next he went into the lead and zinc mining business in Commerce, Oklahoma, with two men he had known a long time. They formed the TCH Mining Company. None of the partners knew much about mining, nor were they able to be at the mine full-time to supervise operations. Harry and his partner Tom Hughes tried to operate the mine in Oklahoma and farm their neighboring properties in Missouri at the same time. Mine machinery broke. Metal prices went down. The third partner, Jerry Culbertson, could not raise enough additional money to keep the mine operating. Harry lost about eleven thousand dollars.

In 1916, Harry was able to borrow money from his mother, who mortgaged more of her land to help him. He went into the oil business with Hughes, Culbertson, and an oil speculator named David H. Morgan. They began selling shares of stock in their Morgan Oil Company to raise money to buy oil leases in Texas, Oklahoma, and Kansas. Bess Wallace even bought some of the stock, and she was just one of many investors. Harry Truman's future looked promising at last. Bess and Harry began to make wedding plans.

On April 6, 1917, the U.S. Congress declared war on Germany. The United States joined with France, Italy, Russia, Britain, and their allies in fighting World War I, which had begun in 1914. Everything was mobilized for the war effort. Morgan Oil Company could not get men or equipment to continue drilling in the oil fields. The company's stock became almost worthless. Somehow, Harry did not seem to care much. The war gave Harry the chance to live out the dream he had had since childhood. Nothing was going to stop him this time. Not his age. Not family obligations. Not even his love for Bess Wallace.

Chapter 3

Captain Harry

War! It changed everyone's life, especially Harry Truman's. He was thirty-three years old. He would not have been among the first to be drafted into the United States military services. As a farmer, he could easily have claimed a deferment. His eyesight also would have prevented him from ever being called up. But Truman wanted to fight for his country.

He had let his enlistment in the Missouri National Guard lapse in 1911. His work on the farm had not allowed him time to attend weekly drills in Kansas City and summer encampments. But when war was declared, he reenlisted in the guard on June 22, 1917. He passed the physical examination despite his poor eyesight because the guard needed men.

He left his sister and mother in charge of the farm with the help of a hired man. Truman lived in a tent city opposite the Kansas City Convention Hall. His job was to recruit men. He told them that if they enlisted in the artillery they would never have to walk. He signed up so many men, he was elected first lieutenant of Battery F. His old rank had been sergeant.

Lieutenant Truman did not tell Bess Wallace about his

reenlistment until after he had done it. Bess was crushed. His business failures had kept them from marrying; now the war did. However, they did announce their engagement, at last.

On August 5, 1917, the Missouri National Guard was called up into the regular United States Army. It became the Second Missouri Field Artillery, part of the 35th Division. It was called the Santa Fe Division and used as its insignia a cross on a wagon wheel. The same sign once marked the old Santa Fe Trail. Truman and his comrades were sent to Camp Doniphan at Fort Sill, Oklahoma. Life was awful at Camp Doniphan. The water was polluted. The men did not have enough tents to live in. Oklahoma dust storms raged much of the time. Terrible illnesses including smallpox swept the camp, killing many men.

Lieutenant Truman had to try to train his men under these unlivable conditions. In addition, he was ordered to organize a canteen for his regiment to make the soldiers' lives a little more bearable. Although Truman had experience in bookkeeping, he did not know anything about running a store. But he knew someone who did—Sergeant Edward Jacobson, who had worked at a clothing store in Kansas City when Truman worked at the Commerce Bank. The canteen sold extra clothing not supplied by the army, cigarettes, stationery, and other supplies. Eddie Jacobson tailored the ill-fitting uniforms. Truman rounded up soldiers who had been barbers in civilian life so that his canteen could offer haircuts.

The most popular thing the canteen sold was gallons and gallons of apple juice to soldiers with mouths, noses, and eyes full of Oklahoma dust. The canteen soon attracted customers from other regiments. Lieutenant Truman and

World War I soldiers at a training camp in the United States. Here they are "cleaning" their mess kits by dipping them in hot water.

Sergeant Jacobson made a ten-thousand-dollar profit in six months, though canteens were not intended to make a profit. Lieutenant Truman was promoted to captain.

Captain Truman and a few other officers were sent to France ahead of the rest of the 35th Division to attend artillery school. On March 30 he sailed out of New York Harbor past the Statue of Liberty. He wondered if he would ever see her again. The first thing he had to worry about for thirty days was German submarines torpedoing his ship.

The identification card Captain Harry S. Truman carried during World War I. This is one of the few pictures of Harry Truman without his glasses.

At the artillery school at Montigny-sur-Abbe, he lived in a five-hundred-year-old chateau (castle) with a real moat and beautiful gardens but no heat or hot water. He did not have much time to enjoy the castle. Captain Truman had to learn complicated math—logarithms, trigonometry, square roots, and logistics. The artillery battery officer's job was to figure the target mathematically, order the guns set to fire, and hope to hit it. Artillery commanders had to be exact in their calculations. They had to be sure the shells hit the enemy targets—and did not hit their own advancing infantry, killing and wounding men by "friendly fire."

When the whole 35th Division reached France, Captain Truman rejoined his regiment. On July 10, he was called before the colonel who told him he was giving him command of a battery. This was the promotion Harry Truman had dreamed of. But his happiness turned into the worst scare of his life when he found out he was to be commanding officer of Battery D. The 194 men in that battery were called the "Dizzy D." The stories about them had built up into legends. It was rumored they had drilled a hole in a French railroad tank car loaded with wine. Another story alleged they deliberately stampeded their horses. True or not, they had the reputation as the holy terrors of the army. The men of Battery D were mostly from Kansas City. When Captain Truman faced them for the first time, he looked the men over, then quickly dismissed them. He was too scared to make a speech.

The men of Battery D could not believe that the army, in its stupidity, had assigned as their commander this man with his thick glasses and quiet ways, a man obviously shaking in his boots. They wanted a tough leader they could depend on to lead them into and *out of* battle. They already had rid themselves of four commanding officers in eight months. Captain Harry Truman would be number five.

But whether the boys of Battery D liked him or not, Captain Harry Truman had a job to do and he was going to do it. He gave the maximum punishments to the first men who did not obey orders. But if his men were accused unjustly, he also defended them against superior officers. Day in and day out, he trained the men of Battery D to be one of the most efficient and accurate batteries in the 35th Division. They hit the target with the most accuracy; they learned to load the big guns in record time. The colonels and the generals began to view these rowdies as something more valuable than candidates for the guardhouse.

On August 17, Battery D and their regiment were ordered to the fighting front. They rode to battle on a train. The big guns were loaded on flatcars and the men and horses rode in boxcars that held either eight horses or forty men. They were called "40 and 8s." The horses were as important as the men, for they pulled the guns and equipment. The 194 men of Battery D had 167 horses to load and manage. Under Captain Truman Battery D soon held the record for fastest loading of their equipment onto the train.

They were sent to the Vosges Mountains in northeastern France where the fighting was not heavy. The National Guard units needed some light combat experience. A lieutenant from the French army guided Captain Truman and Battery D to their assigned position on Mount Herrenberg. At 8:00 P.M. on August 26, Battery D had orders to fire with the other batteries of their regiment for exactly thirty-six minutes. Then they were to get off the mountain before the Germans could return their fire. However, the horses had been removed so they would not be spooked by the loud noise of the guns and were not brought back until 9:00 P.M. to drag the guns away.

Battery D was still on Mount Herrenberg when the Germans located them and began firing. The horses bolted; Truman's horse fell on top of him. Someone panicked and shouted for everyone to run. The men started a headlong retreat. Truman, on his feet again, did not move. His eyes turned a steely gray at what he thought was the cowardice of these men who saw themselves as so tough. He unleashed his most colorful railroad-gang cussing at them. The men were so shocked at hearing this tirade from their quiet captain, they came back. Truman started barking orders: Round up the horses. Shoot the badly injured ones. Hitch up the guns. Camouflage the cannons stuck in the mud. Battery D slipped and slid down the mountain under cover of darkness. By dawn, they reached a place of safety. No man was killed or even hurt, but four horses and two big guns were lost.

Captain Truman dreaded facing the colonel. He thought he would be court-martialed. But much to his relief, he learned the same thing had happened to other batteries under fire for the first time. He was told to go back and retrieve his two cannons. Later, the incident was jokingly named the Battle of Who Run. From then on, the men of Battery D followed their "Captain Harry" anywhere. He had led them *out of* battle safely.

In September, Battery D was ordered to take part in the final offensive of the war. The 35th Division moved out of the Vosges Mountains. This time they did not ride in 40 and 8s. For twenty-two nights they marched all night carrying sixty-pound packs on their backs. By day they hid in the woods so German planes could not spot them. The horses were so weak the men could not ride them or even touch the artillery pieces. Captain Truman did all he could to help his men. He pulled them off the road for a few hours rest during the night. If one was injured, Truman walked while the man rode his horse.

When the exhausted men and animals reached the Argonne Forest, they were ordered at once on another forced march to the fighting area. At 4:20 A.M. on September 26, the great battle began. Hundreds of artillery guns in a line stretching for miles were fired. Some men went deaf from the noise. Truman's hearing was permanently affected when a French artillery unit fired over his head. The guns got so hot, they had to be covered with wet rags. When the front-line German defenses were destroyed, the infantry advanced. The big artillery guns followed them, firing over their heads at more German gun placements. It took double teams of horses to pull and men to push the guns through the mud across the battlefield. Wrecked equipment, dead horses, and wounded men lay everywhere. At midday, Captain Truman and some other officers were ordered to scout out ahead. They soon were pinned down in a ditch while the Germans fired machine guns over their heads until darkness allowed them to escape back to their lines.

Battery D went for days without sleep as the fierce battle seesawed back and forth. Once French soldiers retreated right past them yelling, "The Germans are coming." Battery D lowered its guns to fire point-blank at the advancing German infantry, and the men took out their pistols. The Germans never came. Sent out into no man's land to establish an observation post, Truman spotted a German battery. He sent back word for Battery D to destroy it, even though he was under strict orders not to fire unless told to do so by his superiors. A colonel threatened him with a court-martial for disobeying. But Truman was sure he had saved some lives. During the great Battle of the Argonne in eastern France, 1,200,000 American, British, and French soldiers fought; one out of every ten men was killed.

Battery D kept firing until 10:45 in the morning on November 11, 1918. When the armistice came at 11:00, all fighting halted. The world war was over. But Captain Truman and men did not immediately board a 40 and 8 to head for the first ship home. They were in France for five more months while the governments of the United States, France,

U.S. Army engineers get ready to blow up captured large-caliber shells left behind by retreating German troops during the great Battle of the Argonne.

Britain, and Germany began working out a peace treaty. Truman used this time of waiting to travel about France when he could get leave.

On May 3, 1919, much of Kansas City was up before dawn and headed for the train yards. The Second Missouri Field Artillery was coming home. Captain Truman led Battery D in a parade through cheering crowds. He had brought all but six men home safely. Only one of those had died in battle. The men chipped in and presented Captain Harry with a huge silver cup.

Like most men who have lived through a war, Harry Truman would not have taken a million dollars for the experience nor a million dollars to do it over again.

☆ *Chapter 4* ☆

Businessman

On May 6, 1919, Captain Truman was discharged from military service at Camp Dunston, Kansas. He returned to the farm at Grandview to live, but he knew it would not be for long. His delayed marriage to Bess Wallace was scheduled to take place in seven weeks.

War changed Harry Truman as it does most people. He did not want to return to farming. Bess was a town girl and had no intention of living and working on a farm. His sister, Mary Jane, who had run the farm for two years during the war, refused to run it anymore without Truman's help. The farm was in such poor shape, Truman decided to sell all of the equipment and livestock and rent out the land. Furthermore, he deeded his rights to his mother, sister, and brother. He was sure he was out of farming for good.

Harry S. Truman and Elizabeth Virginia ("Bess") Wallace were married on June 28 at 4:00 P.M. in Trinity Episcopal Church in Independence. After a honeymoon to Chicago and Michigan, the couple returned to live with Bess's mother at 219 North Delaware Avenue.

Soon after the Trumans returned from their wedding trip, Eddie Jacobson called Truman. He suggested they open a haberdashery shop and sell high-quality men's clothing. Af-

Harry and Bess Wallace Truman on their wedding day, June 28, 1919, in Independence, Missouri.

ter all, they had made money when they operated their canteen at Camp Doniphan. Pooling their savings and borrowing more from banks, Truman and Jacobson went into partnership. They rented property at 104 West Twelfth Street. Their store was in the heart of the Kansas City business district, directly across the street from the best hotel

Truman and Jacobson Haberdashery. This is the men's clothing store Harry Truman and his war buddy Edward Jacobson owned from 1919 to 1922 in downtown Kansas City, Missouri.

in town. Truman and Jacobson opened for business the last week in November in time for the Christmas trade. Truman did the bookkeeping, and Jacobson purchased $35,000 worth of merchandise to stock the store. With the help of a clerk, they kept the store open from eight in the morning until nine at night, six days a week. In 1920, people had money and returning veterans needed clothes. The store made a good profit its first year.

Truman kept his silver cup from Battery D on display in the store. The men bought ties and shirts when they came

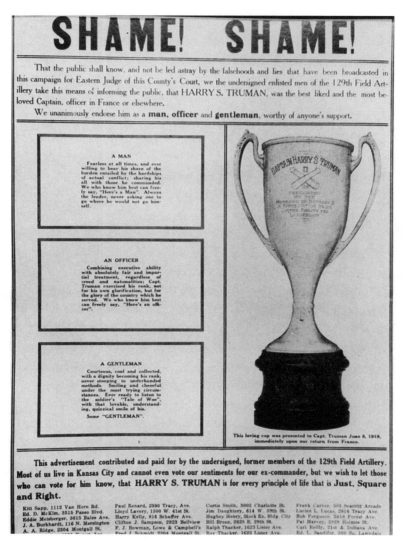

SHAME! SHAME!

That the public shall know, and not be led astray by the falsehoods and lies that have been broadcasted in this campaign for Eastern Judge of this County's Court, we the undersigned enlisted men of the 129th Field Artillery take this means of informing the public, that HARRY S. TRUMAN, was the best liked and the most beloved Captain, officer in France or elsewhere.

We unanimously endorse him as a **man, officer** and **gentleman**, worthy of anyone's support.

A MAN

Fearless at all times, and ever willing to bear his share of the burden entailed by the hardships of actual conflict; sharing his all with those he commanded. We who know him best can freely say, "Here's a Man". Always the leader, never asking one to go where he would not go himself.

AN OFFICER

Combining executive ability with absolutely fair and impartial treatment, regardless of creed and nationalities; Capt. Truman exercised his rank, not for his own glorification, but for the glory of the country which he served. We who know him best can freely say, "Here's an officer".

A GENTLEMAN

Courteous, cool and collected, with a dignity becoming his rank, never stooping to underhanded methods. Smiling and cheerful under the most trying circumstances. Ever ready to listen to the soldier's "Tale of Woe", with that lovable, understanding, quizzical smile of his.

Some "GENTLEMAN".

This loving cup was presented to Capt. Truman June 8, 1919, immediately upon our return from France.

This advertisement contributed and paid for by the undersigned, former members of the 129th Field Artillery. Most of us live in Kansas City and cannot even vote our sentiments for our ex-commander, but we wish to let those who can vote for him know, that HARRY S. TRUMAN is for every principle of life that is Just, Square and Right.

Kitt Sapp, 1112 Van Horn Rd.
Ed. D. McKim, 3515 Paseo Blvd.
Eddie Meisberger, 3615 Bales Ave.
J. A. Burkhardt, 116 N. Merington
A. A. Ridge, 2304 Montgall St.

Paul Renard, 2930 Tracy, Ave.
Lloyd Lavery, 1500 W. 41st St.
Harry Kelly, 816 Schaffer Ave.
Clifton J. Sampson, 2923 Bellview
F. J. Bowman, Lowe & Campbell's
Fred J. Schmidt, 2304 Montgall St.

Curtis Smith, 3002 Charlotte St.
Jim Daughtery, 614 W. 39th St.
Hughey Henry, Stock Ex. Bldg. City
Bill Breen, 2625 E. 29th St.
Ralph Thacker, 1623 Lister Ave.
Roy Thacker, 1623 Lister Ave.

Frank Carver, 503 Scarritt Arcade
Lucien L. Lucas, 2816 Tracy Ave.
Bob Ferguson, 2818 Forest Ave.
Pat Harvey, 2929 Holmes St.
Carl Reilly, 31st & Indiana Ave.
Ed. L. Sandifer, 300 So. Lawndale

Harry Truman's friends from Battery D had this ad printed during Truman's campaign for judge of Jackson County. It shows the cup the men of Battery D presented to him at the end of World War I and tells how highly they thought of him.

to sit around and talk in the evenings. They exchanged news, relived battles, and told one another about job openings. Truman lent some men money to get a start. He was often asked for advice. These men were in their early twenties; Truman was thirty-five. To them, he was mature and wise.

Truman kept up his other contacts with the military. He joined the American Legion and the Veterans of Foreign Wars and remained in the Missouri National Guard. He also joined several Kansas City business clubs. Truman, who had been shunned by boys as a child, was well liked by grown men.

In the election of 1920, Republican Warren G. Harding won the presidency in a landslide by promising a return to prewar normalcy. The 1920s were anything but normal. The Harding administration raised interest rates. Congress raised tariffs on imported goods so high, other countries refused to buy American-made products in return. Farm income dropped by two-thirds; factories closed. The economic downturn was short, but severe.

Men no longer had the money to buy silk shirts and socks. In late 1922, Jacobson and Truman had to go out of business. But the two partners refused to declare bankruptcy, even though they were thousands of dollars in debt. Like his father before him, to Harry Truman a debt was a duty he felt honor bound to pay. Jacobson and Truman talked the businesses and banks to whom they owed money into letting them pay back a little at a time. Truman worked fifteen years to clear those debts. He was left with nothing in the depression of 1921–22, not even the farm.

Chapter 5

His Honor, Judge Truman

Heated political arguments broke out whenever the Young or Truman kinfolks got together. But there was only one political party. They were born and they died Southern Democrats—the party of Andrew Jackson. Loyalty to the Democratic party was not only tradition. It resulted from the long memory of what the family had suffered during the Civil War at the hands of the Republicans—Union soldiers and Jayhawker guerrillas from Kansas. If anyone forgot, Grandmother Harriet Louisa Young, Uncle Harrison, and Mamma Martha Truman reminded them.

Once Harry Truman forgot. In his pride over joining the Missouri National Guard, he wore his blue uniform to the farm one Sunday to show his grandmother. This sweet lady in her eighties turned on her grandson in a fury and ordered him from her house. He was never to return in that blue uniform again as it brought back to his grandmother horrible memories of many blue uniforms in her house forty years before.

Missouri had entered the Union as a slave state in 1821 after a great debate in Congress resulted in the Missouri Compromise. Neighboring Kansas was organized as a territory in 1854. The settlers in Kansas were supposed to decide for themselves whether or not to allow slavery in Kansas. Fighting broke out along the border between Kansas and Missouri in the mid-1850s. Weeks before the Civil War began in 1861, Kansas joined the Union as a free state. Although Missouri was settled mostly by southerners, it voted not to secede from, that is, leave, the Union. Missouri did not join the Confederacy, yet it refused to send troops to the Union (Northern) army. From then on, the state became a battleground between Union and Confederate troops.

While Solomon Young was out west leading wagon trains, again and again soldiers and guerrillas raided the Young farm. They stole or killed livestock. They even took the family silver hidden in the well and anything else they could carry. Union soldiers hanged thirteen-year-old Harrison as a spy and left him for dead as they rode away. Louisa Young managed to cut her son down before he strangled to death. For the rest of his life, Harrison bore the scars of rope burns on his neck. In 1863, the Union army issued infamous Order #11. It forced all residents along the western Missouri border to abandon their homes, which were then looted and burned. Louisa Young, her six children, and twenty thousand other people were sent to "posts," or internment camps, in Kansas City. They had to stay there for over a year.

Even after the war was over, former guerrillas like Jesse and Frank James and the Younger brothers continued to rob trains and banks. For almost twenty years, they caused fear among law-abiding citizens.

Western Missouri, especially Jackson County, became a place divided by loyalty to different factions of the Democratic party. The two main ones in Jackson County were the Pendergast family faction called the Goats and the Shannon faction called the Rabbits. The heads of these factions were often called political bosses. They selected and elected the candidates for political offices from aldermen to governors. Independent candidates had little chance of being elected.

The Trumans and the Youngs were so numerous in Jackson County, they were a political force of their own. When they supported a local candidate, that person usually won. Truman's father was always active in politics. It was one interest both he and his oldest son shared while Harry was growing up. His father often took him to political meetings. At the 1900 Democratic National Convention held in Kansas City, sixteen-year-old Harry had a job as a page. In 1908, John Truman was a delegate to the State Democratic Party Convention. Harry was appointed a clerk at every election in Grandview.

John Truman was loyal to the Pendergast faction, and Harry followed in his footsteps. The elder Truman was rewarded for his loyalty with a job as a county road overseer. When John Truman died, the Pendergasts appointed Harry road overseer in his place. He was also appointed postmaster of Grandview, but he gave his salary to his assistant, a widow supporting a family.

Harry became good friends with Lieutenant James M. Pendergast while they served with the artillery in France. Jim often dropped in at the Truman and Jacobson store. In the summer of 1921, Jim Pendergast and his father, Mike, whom Harry and his father had known a long time, paid him a visit. They asked Harry Truman if he would consider the Democratic nomination to be a judge of the Jackson County Court. Harry told them he might be interested someday. Right then, he had a busy store to manage.

The next spring when he knew the store was going to fail, Harry Truman decided to act on the Pendergast offer. He announced he was going to run for judge of Jackson County. From then until the primary in early August, Truman drove his old Dodge roadster into every township and precinct in the county. He made speeches anyplace he could get someone to listen to him. At a big political picnic, Truman flew overhead in an old Jennie airplane and threw leaflets down on the crowd. By the time the airplane landed, he was airsick, but he marched up to the platform and gave a speech anyway. Harry Truman proved to the Pendergast family he could be a hardworking campaigner.

Harry ran against four other candidates—two independents and two supported by the Shannon faction. He won not because of the Pendergasts' support, but because he had more friends, relatives, and veterans behind him than did any of the other candidates.

Bess Truman's family, the Wallaces, had been in Missouri politics for generations. Her father, David Wallace, had been elected treasurer of Jackson County twice. Her grandfather Benjamin Wallace was once mayor of Independence and a member of the Missouri legislature. William Southern, father of Mrs. Truman's sister-in-law, May Wallace, owned the *Jackson Examiner* newspaper and backed Harry Truman for judge.

Being elected a county judge did not mean Truman became a judge in a court of law. In Missouri, the county court consisted of three judges who were responsible for police protection, highways, and public institutions such as hospitals and orphanages.

When the new court took office, they found the county deeply in debt, by almost $2 million. In two years, $600,000

Judge Harry S. Truman signing county checks with a multiple pen machine.

of this debt was paid off. When Judge Truman ran for re-election in 1924, even Republican newspapers praised his work. The citizens would have reelected him, but the Shannon Rabbits were against him. They teamed up with the Republicans to defeat him.

The Republicans made a sweep of the country, electing a Republican President as well as their candidates in Jackson County. Judge Truman lost the election and was out of work again, with a wife and new baby to support.

Judge Harry S. Truman, with his wife, Bess Truman, and their daughter, Margaret.

The Trumans welcomed a daughter on February 17, 1924. They called her Mary after Harry's sister and Margaret after Bess's mother, but Margie for short. Although Truman respected his father and was in awe of his grandfather, he was closer to his mother and grandmother. He doted on his little sister, Mary Jane, often singing her to sleep when she was a baby and playing piano duets with her as they grew up. The great love of his life was Bess. When little Margie was born, Truman's life was complete. His daughter was truly his pride and joy. Yet much as he deeply loved, respected, and protected the women of his family, he thought equal rights for women were "a lot of hooey."

Truman got a job as sales director of the Kansas City Automobile Club. By the middle 1920s, many people could afford to own cars. But paved roads were few, gas stations were even fewer, and road signs and other services were practically unknown. The Kansas City Automobile Club was one of several clubs formed to help people who wanted to travel by car. Truman sold memberships to his many friends and relatives.

He was also named president of the National Old Trails Association (NOTA), an educational group devoted to preserving the old trails and educating people on their history. What better person for the job than a man who had grown up in the town where the Santa Fe and Oregon trails began, whose grandfather had blazed trails to the West, and whose lifelong hobby was reading history. Truman traveled around the country giving speeches about the old trails.

As if he were not busy enough, Truman thought he ought to get a law degree. Starting in the fall of 1923, he took classes at the Kansas City Law School where he studied under some of the best lawyers and judges in Missouri. However, he gave up his studies after two years. His first love was politics.

The Pendergasts and the Shannons decided to work together after the defeat of their candidates in the 1924 election. Truman knew just the job he wanted—county tax assessor. He would earn a salary of twenty-five thousand dollars a year and could pay off his debts on the haberdashery and his mother's farm. But the Pendergast faction wanted him to run for the court again, this time as presiding judge at a salary of six thousand dollars. Truman could do nothing but agree if he wanted to stay in politics. He won the election easily in 1926.

When Truman returned to the office of judge, he personally visited every mental institution, orphanage, and old people's home run by the county. He fired unnecessary workers to save the county money. He redid the county's taxing process based on one he had seen in Cincinnati. He went to the banks in Chicago and refinanced the county debt at a much lower interest rate.

But after his experience with the Kansas City Auto Club and the NOTA, Truman thought the worst of the bad problems in Jackson County was the roads. He had to weigh down the back of his old Dodge with two bags of cement. Their weight kept him from being thrown through the windshield on roads meant for horses and buggies. The people of the county choked on road dust in summer and got mired in mud up to their running boards in winter. Truman wanted a model road system for Jackson County unlike anything in the United States.

First he persuaded the voters of Jackson County to pass a $7 million bond issue to pay for this plan. He hired the best engineers in the country to lay out 336 miles of roads that would last for many years. By supervising the work carefully, he was able to get 40 extra miles built for the money. When everything was finished, Truman threw a huge barbecue at Sin-A-Bar Farm to celebrate and invited everyone in the county. Thirty-five thousand people showed up. In 1930, Truman was reelected to a third term as judge in appreciation of what he had done for Jackson County.

As Judge Truman and his work became known around Missouri, influential businessmen, veterans, and newspapers began to talk of him as a candidate for governor in the 1932 election. In early 1931, the first Truman for Governor club was formed. But the Pendergasts refused to support him for governor. Harry Truman swallowed his disappointment and campaigned for the new candidate like a loyal Democrat.

But this inspired another dream for Truman—to be a United States congressman. When Missouri was redistricted after the 1930 census, a congressional district was formed in eastern Jackson County. Truman knew he could win it easily with all his Truman, Young, and Wallace relatives voting for him. Tom Pendergast, Jim's uncle and head of the Pendergast faction, said he thought Truman could have the nomination. But then Pendergast changed his mind and gave it to someone else. This time Truman was furious.

It was customary for a presiding judge to hold office no longer than two terms, and Truman was ready to quit in 1934. His father had taught him that holding a public office meant giving the best possible service to the people. (John Truman had died in an on-the-job accident as road overseer trying to build the best road he could.) For eight years people called or came to Harry Truman's home day and night seeking jobs or favors. At one point, someone attempted to kidnap his daughter. Another time, an unknown enemy sent him a poisoned cake. Meanwhile, the Pendergast faction had become associated with increasing violence and dishonesty in Kansas City.

Truman planned to retire to his mother's farm and stay

out of politics. He had done his best. All his dreams seemed to be over. It was a time when the dreams of millions of other Americans also seemed to be over. The United States economy had recovered from the recession of 1921–22 and the "Roaring Twenties" had begun. Business once again flourished. Many of the American people had a wonderful time with new cars, airplanes, new inventions, and great books. But the party had ended with a big bang on October 29, 1929, when the stock market crashed. Why? Again as in 1921, Congress raised tariffs on imported goods. American business people and farmers could not sell their products to other countries. This time there was no quick recovery. Fifteen million people were out of work. Truman joined their ranks in the Great Depression.

☆ *Chapter 6* ☆

Senator Truman

When Truman awoke on the morning of May 8, 1934, he was not even home where his family could wish him a happy fiftieth birthday. Instead, he was alone in a hotel room in Warsaw, Missouri. He was traveling around the state making speeches to help the governor pass a bond issue. Truman's own career in politics would be finished in seven months when his term as presiding judge ran out. Then the phone rang.

On the line were Democratic Party State Chairman James P. Aylward and Truman's old war buddy, Jim Pendergast. They asked Truman to meet them at the Bothwell Hotel in Sedalia, Missouri, right away but refused to explain why. Truman was totally mystified. Out of long friendship with these two men, he agreed to drive to Sedalia.

When he walked into their hotel room, Aylward and Pendergast told him they wanted him to run for the United States Senate. Truman was flabbergasted. Then he said no.

He knew this job had been offered to two other men who had refused it because they knew they could not win. The Democratic primary would be a three-man race against two congressmen, Jacob P. Mulligan and John J. Cochran, who were backed by the St. Louis Democrats.

Aylward and Pendergast talked, pleaded, and banged their fists on the table. They argued that the other Missouri senator, Bennett Clark, was from St. Louis. The state needed a senator from western Missouri. If Mulligan or Cochran were elected, millions of dollars in aid from the federal government might go to the poor people in St. Louis and eastern Missouri. With no one to represent them, western Missouri people suffering in the Great Depression would not get their share.

Truman told them he would prefer to run for governor. That office was more in line with his experience as a judge. But Aylward and Pendergast told him the party needed him to run for the Senate *now*. They guaranteed him all-out support in Kansas City. Truman knew that meant nothing. A Pendergast-backed candidate had lost the last election for senator. Both men appealed to his loyalty to the Democratic party. It was Truman's soft spot. Over and over again he had proved himself a loyal Democrat. He was obliged to prove it one more time. But he tightened his belt; it was going to be a rough ride. Being supported by the Pendergast faction when he ran for office was understood in Jackson County. But in a statewide race for a federal office, that was another story. He would have a lot of explaining to do. On May 14, 1934, Truman announced he was going to run for the Senate.

The words were hardly out of his mouth when the campaign dirty tricks started. The newspapers made fun of him as a country judge who was not even a lawyer. They called him "Pendergast's office boy," who would not have control of his own vote in the Senate should he be elected. His opponents learned Truman still owed money to banks from 1922 when his store failed. This slur backfired in Truman's

The car Harry Truman used during his 1934 campaign to be a U.S. senator from Missouri. He removed the front passenger seat to make room for the microphone and sound equipment he used to make speeches in almost every county of Missouri.

favor. As a judge of Jackson County, he had controlled the spending of millions of dollars for public works. Yet he could not afford to pay off a twelve-year-old debt of nine thousand dollars. This proved he was an honest man.

Since all three candidates were from the big cities, Truman took his campaign to the little towns. Traveling the dusty back roads alone in his Plymouth, he drove himself to exhaustion. On July 6, he collided with another car and

These unemployed workers receive a free meal during the Great Depression. Millions of people were out of work, and those who still had jobs saw their wages fall by 50 percent on the average.

was thrown into the windshield. He broke several ribs, badly bruised his forehead, and sprained his wrist. But he went on campaigning in one hundred degree heat.

Truman shook hands in country stores, talked from the back of farm wagons, anyplace a few people would listen. Often he made as many as twenty speeches a day. Truman's speeches were nothing fancy, just real discussions of problems. Businesses and factories were closed. Banks had failed, causing people to lose their life savings. Many people were out of work. Some people were homeless and starving. Their only food was a bowl of soup and a piece of bread from sidewalk soup kitchens set up by churches and some city governments. Men went door to door selling sewing needles and spools of thread to housewives. Or they peddled apples and pencils on street corners. President Herbert Hoover set up the Reconstruction Finance Corporation to help reopen banks and businesses, but it did not help enough. The Great Depression continued in the United States and all over the world. Truman told his audiences that he was a farmer and a failed businessman, so he understood what they were facing in the terrible depression.

Truman had other people for him, too. The people of Jackson County gave him the campaign slogan "He took Jackson County out of the mud," referring to the road system he had built. He belonged to veterans groups and the Masons. He had been president of the Missouri County Judges Association. This earned him friends among the other judges around the state who would be sure the votes for him were recorded properly and not stolen. He gave his final speech of the primary campaign right in Independence. Then he waited for the votes to come in.

It was a long night. Truman got few votes in St. Louis; his opponents got a few votes in Kansas City. This is what Truman knew would happen. But as the votes slowly were reported from rural counties, the totals for Truman mounted up. He won the Democratic primary by forty thousand votes. In the November election, he was swept into office by a Democratic party landslide across the United States.

On January 3, 1935, Harry S. Truman was escorted to the front of the Senate Chamber in the Capitol in Washington, D.C., by the senior senator from Missouri, Bennett Clark. Vice President John Nance Garner administered the oath of office. Bess and their daughter, Margaret, looked down proudly from the visitors' gallery.

Senator Truman had told the folks back home during the campaign that he was a strong supporter of President Roosevelt and his New Deal programs to help the problems created by the depression. The New Deal promised the three Rs: Relief for the needy; Recovery, so business, factories, and farms could operate again and employ people; and Reform, which encouraged the growth of labor unions and broke the hold of business over its employees by establishing a forty-hour workweek and forty-cents-an-hour minimum wage. President Roosevelt proposed that the federal government should take a much larger role in the life of the nation. The era of big government was on.

Some New Deal programs passed by Congress were unemployment insurance, social security, minimum wages, inheritance taxes, slum clearance, and restrictions on child labor. Roosevelt pushed through public projects to give people work. He had Grand Coulee Dam on the Columbia River built, one of the world's largest projects. He got Congress to pass the Tennessee Valley Authority Act in order to harness the waterpower in rivers by building dams to supply electricity to the southeastern states.

None of the New Deal farm programs seemed to help the farmers enough. Senator Truman's own mother, sister, and brother depended on farm income. He wanted to keep his campaign promise to those people in the rural towns who had voted him into office. He found one way he could help them.

All senators were assigned to committees. Truman became interested in the work of a committee investigating the finances of the railroads. The United States had depended on the railroads for transportation since the Civil War. But the railroads were in trouble in the mid-1930s,

One of the Tennessee Valley Authority dams under construction during the Great Depression. The TVA program provided cheap electric power, made rivers in the area navigable, helped soil and forest conservation, and brought industries and jobs to the region.

and Senator Truman began a program of study, investigation, and hearings to find out why. He discovered the railroads' decline was not the result of the Great Depression but of the greediness of a few rich men who wanted even more millions. These people fired workers and did not spend money to maintain the tracks or equipment. They cut off service to some towns and cities. Accidents increased. This neglect made huge profits possible while putting the railroads on the track to bankruptcy. As a result, the whole country suffered. Truman compared what these men were doing to the way Jesse James used to hold up trains in Missouri.

As he uncovered more and more scandals touching some of the most famous and respected people in the country, Truman was pressured to stop his investigations. He won the respect and admiration of his fellow senators for his determination to keep on. Even when he received a threat that he would be killed on April 22, 1937, he brushed it aside. He said he had survived the worst the Germans could throw at him in 1918; he was not going to let some "nut" bother him. Nevertheless, guards were assigned to protect him.

Senator Truman finished his investigations with a strong speech to Congress about the "legal stealing" from the railroads. For two more years, he worked to pass a transportation law to reform and rebuild the rail lines. Senator Harry Truman became something of a national hero.

This was not his only contribution. He was interested in all kinds of transportation, including the young aviation industry. While conducting the railroad investigations, he found the air transportation industry, too, was in a mess. Senator Truman's investigations led Congress to pass legislation establishing the Civil Aeronautics Board to regulate both private and commercial flying for safer and better service.

But despite his elevation to fame, Senator Truman and his family still had financial problems. He was often called upon to make speeches before important audiences and to endorse products; yet he refused. It would have been perfectly legal and many congressmen did it to supplement their income. But Senator Truman thought he would be selling his office. On his yearly salary of ten thousand dollars, he supported his wife, daughter, mother, mother-in-law, and various relatives from time to time. The Trumans could not afford to live in Washington all year round. They rented a tiny furnished apartment from January to June; the rest of the year Mrs. Truman and their daughter went home to Independence.

Senator Truman often had to stay on alone in Washington, moving to a hotel if Congress was still in session. The first summer he was alone in Washington, he wrote to his wife, "Dear Bess: You don't know how much I appreciated the letter that came in this morning's mail. I was so devilishly homesick. . . . Kiss Margie and tell her to write me a letter. . . ."

Margaret Truman had to go to two schools a year—one in Independence from September until Christmas and one in Washington from January to June. Not being able to afford living in Washington all year also meant packing up twice a year and driving halfway across the country on two-lane roads. The trip took almost a week in each direction, even though the senator was a fast driver. Despite these hardships, Senator Truman wanted to run for reelection when his term was up in 1940. He had worked very hard, yet he thought there was still more to do. But President Roosevelt had other ideas.

Roosevelt decided to start a public crusade against political organizations called machines. The machine bosses got rich from skimming off tax money into their own pockets. A depression was going on and people were angry as they were out of work and losing their homes because they could not pay the high taxes. Machine bosses in many large American cities not only got their choices for aldermen and governors elected, they also had helped elect Roosevelt himself in 1932.

But Roosevelt no longer needed the big city bosses and their machines after his huge win of a second term in the 1936 elections. He instructed Maurice Mulligan, federal district attorney in Kansas City, to begin prosecuting Tom Pendergast, boss of the Kansas City machine. He sent the Federal Bureau of Investigation, Treasury agents, and other government investigators to help. Tom Pendergast was indicted in April 1939 and pleaded guilty to evading $1 million in income taxes. He was sentenced to fifteen months in jail and five years' probation, during which time he had to stay away from politics.

Harry Truman could not believe this was happening. It meant his support for the 1940 election was gone. He went from the heights of public opinion to the depths. Throughout the whole Pendergast investigation, no one discovered anything dishonest about Truman. Still, he suffered from guilt by association, especially when, unlike Tom Pendergast's other associates, Truman refused to turn against him. Right or wrong, Truman strongly believed in being loyal to his friends, and he expected them to be loyal to him. It was a virtue that sometimes became a damaging blind spot in his life. The newspapers said he should resign from office, and Truman considered it. He thought about quitting the Senate and going back into the army as a colonel in the field artillery. But at fifty-six, he was told he was too old.

President Roosevelt offered him a job on the Interstate Commerce Commission if he would not run again. Senator Truman had always supported President Roosevelt and his New Deal programs, but he was enraged by Roosevelt's proposal. Truman sent back word, no thanks. He was going to run again to fight for his good name, even if the only vote he got was his own.

He called a meeting of his friends in St. Louis to discuss his reelection. Those men that came all advised him not to run. The obstacles were too great. Worst of all, the popular President Roosevelt appeared to support his opponent, Missouri Governor Lloyd Stark.

Senator Truman refused to give up. He kicked off his campaign with a big rally June 15, 1940, in Sedalia, Missouri, right in the center of the state. Some four thousand people friendly to him were there. Bess, Margaret, and his mother were beside him. When Senator Truman got up to speak, he talked of equal opportunities for everyone. He said, "I believe in the brotherhood of man; not merely the brotherhood of white men, but the brotherhood of all men before the law." No black people were in the crowd listening to him. But there were people whose grandparents had once owned slaves. Mob violence and lynchings still occurred in Missouri against black people. But Harry Truman thought the Constitution gave equal rights and equal protection to everyone. He was not afraid to say so even if it could cost him the election.

With all the big-city newspapers against him, Harry Truman's best hope for reelection rested again with the rural people. He had no money to put up big signs or buy time on the radio to push his campaign. He drove into 75 of the 114 counties in Missouri to talk to the voters personally. His speeches centered on his accomplishments as a judge and a senator. Then he talked about what he wanted to do in the future for people.

Many senators from other states respected Truman's work and wanted to see him reelected. They offered to come to

Missouri to campaign for him. Some sent letters of endorsement, which Truman printed and passed out. The military veterans and Missouri guardsmen supported him. So did the railroad workers who had regained jobs because of the Truman Transportation Bill.

Still, on election night, the prospects for a Truman win looked poor. He was 11,000 votes behind when he went to bed at eleven o'clock. A St. Louis newspaper printed headlines saying he had been defeated. By the next morning, Senator Truman was 8,800 votes ahead.

The cost of Truman's do-it-yourself campaign was $21,000. Few people gave money to his campaign since almost no one thought he would win. He had to borrow $3,500 on his life insurance to pay expenses. During the election campaign, the Republicans foreclosed on the long-standing mortgage on Blue Ridge Farm. Martha Truman, eighty-eight years old, had lived there most of her life. For the second time, she was driven from her home by Republicans—the first time by Union soldiers, the second time by politicians. Her oldest son, the senator, had no money to help her. Harry and Vivian rented a little house for her in the town of Grandview where she soon fell and broke her hip. The family always blamed the dirty campaign tricks of the Republicans for this accident.

The day after the November election, the senator went right back to Washington. The Congress was still in session. When Harry S. Truman walked into the Senate, his fellow senators of both parties gave him a standing ovation.

☆ *Chapter 7* ☆

Mr. Vice President

Harry Truman's second term as a United States senator began officially January 3, 1941, and he knew exactly what his mission had to be. When Adolph Hitler and Germany started World War II in September 1939, the United States was totally unprepared for war. The scramble to build military camps, factories, ships, and planes resulted in a great waste of money and raw materials. The U.S. government spent many times what projects should have cost and did not get the taxpayers' money's worth in return: airplanes that crashed, army camp sewer systems that didn't work, steel plates on the hulls of ships that could not withstand storms. Men died needlessly while other Americans got rich. During 1940, even though he faced almost certain defeat in the fall election, Harry Truman had tried to do one more service for his country. He drove his old car thirty thousand miles from Washington, D.C., south to Florida and Texas, north to Wisconsin and Michigan, and out west visiting defense projects. He did not tell anyone who he was. His years of experience as a judge in Jackson County and as an army officer made Harry Truman an expert in spotting fraud. When he returned to Washington, D.C., he warned the

War Department about what he had seen, but they did nothing about it.

Harry Truman took charge. In February 1941, he made a speech to the Senate telling of the disgraceful abuses he had found in his travels. He pleaded for funds for a special investigating committee. Surprisingly, the Senate was reluctant to grant funds. When word of what Truman wanted to do reached representatives of big business, they pressured their senators not to vote for the investigation. But Harry Truman appealed to the senators' patriotism, and the Senate finally voted a token fifteen thousand dollars to start his work. Truman and six other senators held the first hearings of the Committee to Investigate the National Defense Program on April 15, 1941. The purpose of the committee's work was to see that each tax dollar spent for the defense effort bought a full dollar's worth of labor or war materials.

What Harry Truman found made him sick and ashamed of some of his fellow Americans. Businesses fought their own wars by trying to hog scarce raw materials so they could make big profits on government contracts and force their competition to go broke. Labor often staged strikes demanding big wage increases, although what they were working on was critical to the defense effort. The senator called the presidents of the largest companies and heads of the biggest unions before his committee for questioning. Generals, admirals, and government bureaucrats squirmed when the senators asked why they *wasted* supplies.

Truman began giving talks on the radio so people would know what was going on. Newspapers reported more and more on his work; his picture was on the cover of *Time* magazine. The committee held hearings not only in Washington, D.C., but also in other cities around the country.

Senator Harry S. Truman (center) on the Senate committee investigating the national defense program.

Senator Truman traveled constantly. Bess Truman ran her husband's Senate office while he was gone.

On Sunday, December 7, 1941, Senator Truman was resting for the day at a hotel in Columbia, Missouri. His wife called to tell him shocking news. The Japanese had attacked Pearl Harbor, Hawaii, without warning. It was only later, however, that the public learned how devastating the destruction to the army and navy was: four U.S. battleships sunk; four more heavily damaged; 240 planes destroyed on the ground; 2,400 men killed and 1,300 wounded.

Senator Truman raced to an airfield and chartered a small plane to fly him to St. Louis. Once there, he boarded a commercial airliner for Washington, D.C. Harry Truman reached the Capitol just in time to hear President Roosevelt

"A day of infamy." The surprise attack on Pearl Harbor by the Japanese took place on December 7, 1941. Left to right: Battleships USS *West Virginia* and USS *Tennessee* are badly damaged. USS *Arizona* is sunk, entombing 1,200 men.

address a joint session of Congress. "Yesterday December 7, 1941—a date which will live in infamy—the United States of America was suddenly and deliberately attacked by naval and air forces of the Empire of Japan." Roosevelt asked the Congress for a declaration of war, and every member of Congress except one voted for it. On December 11, Germany and Italy declared war on the United States.

The United States was helpless to stop Japan as its war machine quickly rolled over the Philippine Islands, Hong Kong, Singapore, Indochina, and Burma. In a few months the Japanese were ready to invade Australia.

Even with U.S. soldiers dying by the thousands, Senator Truman still found some business and labor leaders who did not seem to care. His committee relentlessly kept on with its investigations. The work of the Truman Committee, as it came to be called, was known in every household in the country. Crooked contractors not only had contracts canceled, but they also had to pay back money they had overcharged the government. When labor unions went on strike, the government sometimes seized the industry and operated it. The Truman Committee was estimated to have saved the taxpayers $10 billion to $15 billion.

Senator Truman began to hear his name mentioned, among others, as a candidate for vice president in the 1944 election. He tried to discourage this idea in every way he knew. When he went to the Democratic National Convention in Chicago in August 1944, he even agreed to nominate someone else for vice president. Much to his despair, more and more delegates wanted him. Still, he said no.

On Thursday afternoon of the convention, Robert Hannegan, chairman of the Democratic party and a fellow Missourian, called Senator Truman to his hotel room. Most of the Democratic party leaders were present. Hannegan told Truman he was President Roosevelt's choice for vice president. Truman did not believe him even after Hannegan showed him a note from Roosevelt. Finally, in desperation, Hannegan put through a telephone call to Roosevelt in San Diego, California. Truman heard President Roosevelt's booming voice say Senator Truman was his choice.

At first, Truman was completely stunned. Then he got angry. "Well, if that is the situation, I'll have to say yes, but why the hell didn't he tell me in the first place."

Senator Truman reluctantly resigned from his committee in early August. He hated to leave, as much work still needed

A collection of Truman campaign literature. The poster of President Franklin Delano Roosevelt and Senator Harry S. Truman was used during the 1944 election campaign.

to be done. But he would not have time to work on the committee anymore.

The next week he met with President Roosevelt at the White House for lunch. The President told him that he had no time to campaign personally. Harry Truman would have to campaign for both of them. Roosevelt had to devote all his time and energy to the conduct of the war. Truman thought the President did not seem in good health as Roosevelt's hands shook, his voice was weak, and he was thin and pale. Franklin Roosevelt had contracted polio when he was thirty-nine years old and had to wear heavy leg braces to stand. The rest of the time he was in a wheelchair.

Harry Truman kicked off the campaign at Lamar, Missouri, his birthplace. He enjoyed this campaign. The Democratic ticket of Roosevelt and Truman won easily against Thomas Dewey, the Republican candidate. Dewey was the popular, forty-two-year-old governor of New York. But the Republicans could only say it was "time for a change after twelve years of the New Deal." The voters did not want to change presidents in the middle of a world war.

Because of the war, a quiet inauguration ceremony was held on the south portico of the White House on January 20, 1945. Mr. Truman stood beside Franklin Delano Roosevelt to be sworn in. Almost eight thousand people, including a few hundred Missourians, stood ankle deep in slushy snow on the White House lawn. Harry Truman was the first person from Missouri to be elected vice president.

He was in office only a week when he created a terrible storm of criticism. On January 26, Tom Pendergast died in Kansas City. Vice President of the United States Harry S. Truman went to his funeral. The press rehashed all the old Pendergast scandals; it was 1940 all over again. By the time they were through, the American people's respect for their new vice president all but disappeared, his work on the Truman Committee forgotten. Harry Truman knew this would happen if he went, but loyalty ruled his feelings. Even though Tom Pendergast died an ex-convict, he had been a political friend. To Harry Truman, the *right* thing to do was be there to say good-bye.

President Roosevelt was not in Washington to stop him. Two days after the inauguration, Roosevelt left for Yalta in the southern part of the Soviet Union (sometimes still called Russia, although that is only part of this Communist-run country). There Roosevelt discussed the war with Joseph Stalin, head of the Soviet government, and Winston Churchill, prime minister of Britain. He was gone over a month.

Even when he returned, Vice President Truman seldom saw him. Truman made two official visits to the White House and several unofficial ones. But the vice president was not invited by the President to attend every cabinet meeting and was told little. At the end of March, President Roosevelt, badly in need of rest, left for Warm Springs, Georgia.

Harry Truman went from being a very busy man as senator to twiddling his thumbs as vice president. According to the Constitution, the vice president's only duties are to preside over the Senate and to vote in case of a tie. Any other work he does is up to the President. Thursday, April 12 was a typical day for the vice president. He had breakfast at his apartment on Connecticut Avenue. On his way to the Capitol, he dropped his daughter off at Georgetown University where she was a student. At his office he saw people, dictated some letters, and returned phone calls. At noon, he convened the Senate and presided over it. Members of the Senate talked at length about Mexican water rights on the Colorado River and the Rio Grande. It was not a hotly debated issue, so the vice president had little to do to keep order. As he sat at his desk overlooking the Senate, he began to write one of his almost daily letters to his mother and sister back home in Grandview.

When the Senate adjourned at 4:46 P.M., Vice President Truman went to Speaker of the House Sam Rayburn's office to attend a meeting. It was a rainy, dismal day, and the Capitol was all but deserted. When Truman reached the speaker's office, Rayburn told him there was a call for him from Stephen Early, President Roosevelt's press secretary. Harry Truman immediately returned the call, and Early urged him to come to the White House at once. Vice President Truman dashed out and ran alone through the basement of the Capitol to where his car and driver, Tom Harty, waited.

Harty drove the vice president up to the main entrance of the White House facing Pennsylvania Avenue. Two White House ushers were waiting to open the door of his car. Truman hurried inside and took the elevator to the Roosevelt family's living quarters on the second floor. When he entered Mrs. Roosevelt's study, the first lady was waiting for him.

Eleanor Roosevelt put her hand on his shoulder and said, "Harry, the President is dead."

The vice president could not speak. He could not believe it was true. He had heard the President's health was improving in Warm Springs. But when he looked at Mrs. Roosevelt's sad face, he knew it must be true.

"Is there anything I can do for you?" he asked her.

Eleanor Roosevelt answered, "Is there anything *we* can do for *you*? For you are the one in trouble now."

☆ *Chapter 8* ☆

Mr. President

In that one room of the White House, it was as if the world had come to an end. No one moved. No one said another word. In his mind, Harry Truman tried to come to terms with the terrible news he had just heard. He could not believe Franklin Delano Roosevelt was dead. He did not *want* to believe Harry S. Truman was now President of the United States.

But time had to start again. Mr. Truman knew he could not allow himself the luxury of being overwhelmed by shock and grief. Just as on the day he assumed command of Battery D, he had a job to do and he was going to do it.

Mr. Truman immediately arranged for a plane to take Mrs. Roosevelt to Warm Springs. Then he ordered cabinet members and other government leaders summoned to the White House.

Secretary of State Edward Stettinius arrived in a matter of minutes. It was the secretary's official duty to announce the death of the President and arrange the swearing in of the next President.

Within the hour, cabinet members, leaders of Congress, and presidential assistants crowded into the Cabinet Room of the White House. Truman stood before the fireplace at one end of the room. The clock on the mantle pointed to 7:09. His wife and daughter stood beside him. Chief Justice of the United States Harlan F. Stone took his place facing him. In his left hand, Truman held a Bible. He placed his right hand on top of it.

Justice Stone said, "I, Harry Shippe Truman, ..."

Harry Truman repeated, "I, Harry S. Truman, do solemnly swear that I will faithfully execute the Office of the President of the United States, and will to the best of my ability, preserve, protect, and defend the Constitution of the United States." These are the exact words as written in the U.S. Constitution. Then he added as George Washington had, "So help me God" and kissed the Bible.

After the official photographs were taken, Harry Truman asked the cabinet officers to remain. Everyone else quietly left. There were no speeches, no celebrations, no congratulations for the new President of the United States.

Even before the important cabinet meeting could begin, Mr. Truman had to make decisions. Newspaper and radio reporters wanted to know if the international conference to write a charter forming the United Nations would still take place April 25 in San Francisco, California. When President Roosevelt was at Yalta two months before, the United States, the Soviet Union, Britain, and China had invited forty-one other countries to the San Francisco conference. Many thought the future peace of the world depended on the establishment of a United Nations organization. Yes, President Truman announced, the UN Conference would go on as planned.

Then he began his first meeting with the cabinet. The cabinet is made up of people appointed by the President to head various departments of government such as the De-

Harry S. Truman takes the oath of office in the Cabinet Room of the White House at 7:09 P.M., April 12, 1945. His hand is on the Bible as Chief Justice of the United States Harlan F. Stone administers the oath. Mrs. Bess Truman looks on. The portrait is of President Woodrow Wilson.

partments of War (now called the Defense Department), the Treasury, the State Department, the Interior Department, and others. Cabinet members usually offer their resignations as a courtesy when a new President comes into office. Harry Truman asked all the cabinet members to keep their posts. He intended to continue the policies of the late President, and he needed their help to get through the emergency created by Roosevelt's sudden death. He knew what some were thinking: Since Roosevelt was elected to the office four times, it seemed he would always be President. No man could take his place. Truman could not help thinking the same thing himself. But for a world war to be won and the United States to move forward, the ghost of Roosevelt could not govern. Harry Truman was President now and he would make the decisions.

After the cabinet meeting, Secretary of War Henry L. Stimson stayed behind to speak to the new President on an urgent matter. Stimson reminded Mr. Truman that he once had come to see him when Truman headed the Senate committee investigating defense contracts. At that time the secretary had pleaded with Truman, then still a senator, to drop one of his investigations into a most important war project that had to remain top secret. Now Stimson told Truman that the project was an extremely powerful explosive. But he did not explain it fully nor did he call it the atomic bomb. Mr. Truman was puzzled and shook his head; this was one more thing Franklin Roosevelt had not told his vice president about. Harry Truman knew he had to educate himself on many things quickly, including this supersecret, mysterious weapon.

But he could not read or listen to any more that night. He was so tired, he went home. The new President ate a ham-and-turkey sandwich and drank a glass of milk. Then he called his mother in Grandview and went to bed. The next day was Friday, the thirteenth. He knew it was going to be a "dinger."

At 9:00 A.M. sharp, President Truman arrived at the White House. He met with Secretary of State Stettinius at 10:15. Together they drew up a Proclamation of Mourning for President Roosevelt. It was the first official paper Harry Truman signed as President. At 10:53, he met with the secretaries of the Navy and War and the Joint Chiefs of Staff, who gave him a gloomy report. They expected the war in Europe to last another six months, the war with Japan another year and a half.

At noon, the new President drove to the Capitol for a surprise visit. Senators, representatives, even Senate pages came by to shake his hand and give him their best wishes. This gesture of Truman's showed he hoped for good relations between the President and the Congress. At lunch with sixteen senators and representatives, he told them he intended to address a joint session of Congress and the people of the United States at 1:00 P.M. on Monday, April 16. The American people were frightened when Franklin Roosevelt died. Many people were devoted to him. Even many of those who disagreed with his policies saw him as a father figure. To have their "father" die in the middle of a desperate war was frightening. Harry Truman had to comfort a grieving nation and make them believe he could be a strong President and world leader.

It was a sad weekend as the Roosevelt family, the nation, and the new President laid the former President to rest in the rose garden at Roosevelt's ancestral home, Hyde Park, on the Hudson River in New York State.

On Monday, the new President told the country he had always supported the policies of Franklin Roosevelt. He said, "Tragic fate has thrust upon us grave responsibilities. We must carry on. Our departed leader never looked backward. He looked forward and moved forward. This is what he would want us to do. That is what America will do. . . . Our demand has been, and it remains—unconditional surrender!" This statement brought a standing ovation in the Congress. He added that he had full confidence in the U.S.

commanders like General Douglas MacArthur in the Pacific and General Dwight Eisenhower in Europe to win the war. He asked for everyone's support, and he earnestly prayed for God's help. Members of Congress and the people seemed to feel better after they heard Truman talk. He had passed his first test as President.

That evening President Truman took time out to write a letter to his mother and sister. He told them of the momentous events that had occurred since five o'clock Thursday afternoon, April 12. He closed the letter this way: "My greatest trial was today when I addressed the Congress. It seemed to go over all right, from the ovation I received. Things have gone so well that I'm almost as scared as I was Thursday when Mrs. R. told me what had happened. Maybe it will come out all right.

"Soon as we get settled in the White House you'll both be here to visit us. Lots of love from your very much worried son and bro[ther]. Harry"

Within days Harry Truman saw he had to surround himself with his own team. He began replacing staff members who still referred to Roosevelt as *The President.* The day after his first press conference he asked Charles Ross, his boyhood friend, to become his press secretary. He also invited Harry Vaughan from the Missouri Army Reserve to be his military aide and Eddie McKim of Battery D to help him. President Truman needed some men around him who thought and talked Missourian.

One of his old Missouri friends gave him a brass sign set in a walnut base that said in black letters, "I'm from Missouri" on one said. The other side said, "The buck stops here." Mr. Truman took a fancy to it and kept it on his desk in the Oval Office of the White House. The term was used in old wild West poker games. It referred to the person dealing the cards. President Truman used the saying in several speeches. Presidents since Truman have used it, too. It has come to mean that a person accepts final responsibility.

The Joint Chiefs of Staff were wrong about how long the war in Europe would last. Germany began to fall apart quickly. Twelve days after he took office Harry Truman learned the German government had approached Sweden about surrendering. On April 28, the German army in Italy did surrender. On May 1, the German government announced that Adolph Hitler was dead. A week later, Harry Truman woke up after sleeping his first night in the White House to find his sixty-first birthday, May 8, 1945, was the long-awaited V-E Day, Victory in Europe. But in his announcement of the end of the war in Europe, he reminded the celebrating people it was only half a victory. The greatest and costliest struggle lay ahead.

The Japanese still held large areas of Asia. The war lords of Japan stubbornly refused to consider that they could lose. The United States and Britain saw the only way to victory was to invade Japan itself. Immediately after V-E Day, the Army Air Force's B-17 and B-24 bombers were ordered out of Europe to the Pacific theater of war. Soldiers not needed for the occupation force in Europe were given short leaves at home before being sent to fight again in the Pacific. A million troops waited to begin Operation Olympic; the invasion was scheduled for November. The president and his admirals and generals knew the cost in lives would be extremely high.

The American forces had pushed back the Japanese island by island all the way from Australia to Okinawa, south of Japan itself. But they paid a terrible price. American soldiers, sailors, and marines killed or wounded often ran 35 percent or higher for each island taken. The Japanese were fanatic fighters, blowing themselves up with hand grenades rather than surrendering. Japan still had millions of crack troops willing to die for their emperor.

The United States and Britain needed the Soviet Union to enter the war against Japan. This action would force Japan to keep a million of its troops in Manchuria, which lay between the Soviet Union and the rest of China. These Japanese troops could not be used against the American and British troops during the invasion, thus saving thousands of lives.

During the short time since the Yalta conference, Joseph Stalin had broken many of the agreements made there. He refused to withdraw Russian troops from any territory they had captured. He tried to take over part of northern Italy. He would not allow free elections in Poland as he promised, preferring to keep the temporary Polish government that leaned toward communism. Stalin had his eyes on Belgium, Greece, Turkey, Lebanon, and Syria. Communist governments were already installed in Yugoslavia as well as in Bulgaria, Rumania, and Hungary.

Winston Churchill feared that if the Soviet Union did not fight the Japanese, Russian armies would grab all of Europe as far as the English Channel and Spain. The Americans and the British would be too busy invading Japan to stop Stalin. Churchill urged another meeting between himself, Stalin, and the new American President to stop the Soviet takeover in Europe and to make sure the Soviet Union would declare war on Japan. The three leaders agreed to meet at Potsdam near Berlin in July 1945.

When Truman met Winston Churchill for the first time,

The meeting at Potsdam, Germany, in July 1945 between (left to right) Prime Minister Winston Churchill of Britain, President Harry S. Truman of the United States, and Premier Joseph Stalin of the Soviet Union.

he liked him immediately, although he found him a little too talkative. Joseph Stalin was several days late because he had suffered a mild heart attack. Truman was surprised to find he liked him, too.

At their first formal meeting, Stalin suggested Truman preside. During the conference, Truman tried to stop Stalin from grabbing countries and from demanding billions in war reparations from other countries not only defeated, but starving. In Hungary, Russian soldiers forced the president of the largest bank to carry bags of gold from the vault and load it on Russian trucks for two days and nights. When the Soviet Union could not get gold from defeated countries, Russian soldiers dismantled factories and hauled them away to the Soviet Union.

Little was accomplished at Potsdam. Stalin promised to declare war on Japan August 15. But after seeing what the Soviet Union was doing in Europe, Truman decided Stalin would have no say in the occupation of Japan. He saw that the Soviet Union was planning to take over the world and convert it to communism.

By the end of the conference, President Truman no longer needed the Soviet Union to fight Japan. On July 16, the day after he reached Potsdam, he was notified that the atomic bomb had been tested successfully in a remote place in New Mexico. It was the result of years of round-the-clock work by British and American scientists at a cost of $2.5 billion. The development of the atomic bomb began as a race by the British against the Germans, who were trying to make an atomic weapon to put on their V-1 and V-2 rockets. If Hitler had developed an atomic weapon first, he would have enslaved the entire world. But the Germans had not been able to make a bomb before they were defeated.

Before the atomic bomb was tested, no one had any idea of its devastating far-reaching and long-term effects. Many experts thought it would be a dud or maybe somewhat more powerful than a regular bomb. It was only half the size of conventional bombs. Therefore, the first bomb was exploded not from a plane but on a 100-foot tower. The flash of the explosion on July 16 could be seen two hundred miles away in Santa Fe and Albuquerque, New Mexico, and in El Paso, Texas. Its sound waves broke windows a hundred miles away. The U.S. government had to quickly give out the explanation that an ammunition dump had blown up accidentally.

President Truman was not ready to use the bomb against the Japanese, although Churchill urged him to do so. Stalin pretended not to understand what Truman was talking about at Potsdam when he told him about the bomb. President Truman conferred with his military and civilian advisers. They agreed that to defeat Japan, they had three choices. The first choice was to bomb and blockade. The U.S. forces had relentlessly bombed Japanese cities, and submarines had blocked all the ports. The war could go on like this for years and would cause more Japanese deaths than the atomic bomb. The second choice was to invade Japan itself. This meant a million Americans would face over 2 million Japanese troops. Plus a fanatic Japanese civilian population had been built up into a national volunteer army to defend their homeland. The third choice was to use the atomic bomb.

At first Harry Truman hoped that a demonstration of the bomb's power by exploding it over some remote deserted island would convince the Japanese to end the war. But scientists and generals argued that there were only three bombs in existence. One was used in testing. If the second were wasted in a demonstration that might not impress the Japanese militarists, only one would be left to use directly against Japan itself. By that time, Japanese spies would know there were no more bombs and the war would go on.

On July 26 from Potsdam, the United States, Britain, and China (the Soviet Union was not at war with the Japanese) sent an ultimatum to Japan to surrender. Not trusting the Japanese government to tell their people about this offer, Truman had 27 million leaflets dropped over Japan. The Japanese government did not even bother to reply officially to the proposal. Japanese Radio Tokyo on July 28 said that the Potsdam Proclamation was "unworthy of consideration" and "absurd" and that Japan would fight on.

Truman consulted 150 of the country's leading scientists. Almost all of them urged him to use the bomb. So did his military advisers, who said it would save a million casualties on both sides if it avoided the invasion of the Japanese mainland.

In the end, the decision was Harry Truman's alone. He said many times he thought the *right* thing to do was use the atomic bomb to save the most lives. Yet people will argue, debate, and some will condemn Harry Truman's decision for decades, maybe centuries.

President Truman ordered that the atomic bomb had to be used according to the laws of war. It could be dropped only on military targets. His advisers drew up a list of four Japanese cities that were considered military targets. General Carl Spaatz of the 20th Air Force in the Pacific was ordered to use a B-29 airplane to deliver the bomb. This was to be done sometime after August 3, whenever weather conditions permitted flying the mission. To assemble the bomb, planes and ships rushed the parts to Tinian Island near Guam in the Pacific Ocean. On August 6, 1945, the "Little Boy," code name for the bomb, was dropped on Hiroshima, Japan. It was exploded 1,800 feet in the air. Four-and-a-half square miles of the city were destroyed. About 92,000 people were believed killed on that day. Some were never found. Thousands died later from the radiation.

The President was aboard the navy cruiser *Augusta* on his way home from Potsdam when he received the news. Again he issued a statement to the Japanese to surrender and ordered leaflets scattered over Japan. He waited three days, but the Japanese would not surrender. On August 9, he ordered the second and last bomb dropped. This time the weather was clear over Nagasaki. About 40,000 people

In the background on the left stands one of the few large buildings still standing in Hiroshima after the atomic bomb was dropped. It is the city's largest department store. In front are the melted and twisted steel beams that were all that remained of a large movie theater.

died immediately. That same day, the Soviet Union declared war on Japan.

The next day, the Japanese government sent messages through Sweden and Switzerland that they would accept the terms of the Potsdam Proclamation. Their only condition was that they be allowed to retain their emperor, Hirohito, as their ruler. President Truman consulted with Britain, China, and the Soviet Union. Four days later, he replied that the emperor could stay but would have no power. The Japanese surrendered.

President Truman decided the formal surrender of the

"The day of retribution." Japanese Premier Shigemitsu signs the formal documents of surrender ending World War II. The ceremony is aboard the battleship USS *Missouri* in Tokyo Bay on September 2, 1945.

Japanese would take place aboard the battleship, USS *Missouri*. His daughter, Margaret, had launched the "Mighty Mo" in January 1944, and Truman had made a speech at the ceremonies.

The *Missouri* steamed into Tokyo Bay surrounded by other battleships, aircraft carriers, cruisers, destroyers, and submarines. Wave after wave of army and navy planes flew low overhead. By this display of power in their own capital city, President Truman hoped to drive home to the fanatic Japanese that they had really lost the war. At 9:00 A.M. on Sunday, September 2, 1945, representatives of the Japanese government dressed in formal clothes came aboard the *Missouri* to sign the surrender. To insult them, General Douglas MacArthur and other high officers of the United States and its allies were not in dress uniforms but wore everyday khaki pants, shirts, and no ties.

The actual signing of the surrender documents was broadcast live around the world. Afterward, President Truman spoke over the radio. He thanked the servicemen and women and all the American people for their sacrifices and efforts to win the war. Proclaiming the day as V-J Day, he said, "It is a day which we Americans shall always remember as a day of retribution—as we remember that other day, the day of infamy." World War II was over. Thirty million people had died in six years.

☆ *Chapter 9* ☆

Winning the Peace

In the momentous four months after Harry Truman became President, Germany surrendered in May; the United Nations was established in June; the Potsdam Conference took place in July; the atomic bombs were dropped and Japan surrendered in August. But winning the peace brought President Truman more problems than winning the war.

The American people were exhausted by government controls, rationing, and shortages of everything from doctors to nylons. Juvenile delinquency was widespread because fathers were away fighting, and mothers and grandparents had to replace men in factories, stores, and offices. Worst of all was the tragedy of dead, wounded, or captured men in every family. Yet once the fighting ended, people feared a return of the dread Great Depression. Factories would stop making planes, ships, and tanks and then would lay off workers. Women would return to their kitchens. Older people would go back into retirement. Eight million men and two hundred thousand women would leave military service. Where were people to find jobs?

Four days after V-J Day, President Truman sent Congress a twenty-one point program. He hoped it would help the American economy go from war to peace without the return of the depression. He called it his Economic Bill of Rights—the Fair Deal. He proposed a right-to-work law for full employment even if it meant the United States government had to provide the jobs. Along with jobs, he insisted on fair employment practices to insure equal job opportunities for everyone, regardless of race, religion, or color. He urged increases in minimum wage and longer unemployment pay. A million-and-a-half housing units were desperately needed by men and women returning to civilian life. This was an urgent problem. Truman pushed and pushed Congress until federally financed construction bills were passed in 1948 and 1949. President Truman was years ahead of his time in wanting a national health program, aid to education, and increased Social Security payments.

Harry Truman was very proud of his Fair Deal. He saw that the war had changed the world and its people forever. There was no going back to the way life was in the 1930s, and Truman felt new times required new ideas. However, Congress said Truman's program was too new, too far-reaching. Few of the Fair Deal's twenty-one points became law during Truman's presidency. But he sowed the seeds that would flower in the future.

While Congress debated the Fair Deal, they saw the Great Depression was not going to return. The pentup demand for a million-and-a-half new houses, new cars, new washing machines, and thousands of other items that had not been manufactured during the war sent the economy into a boom. But President Truman was wary. He had seen his haberdashery business go from boom to bust overnight after World War I. He did all he could to prevent the same thing from happening after World War II.

Owing to the shortage of workers during the war, labor

unions had become strong. A serious threat to the galloping postwar economy was widespread strikes of the unions in many industries. To prevent hardship on the public because of strikes, the President established committees to investigate each labor dispute. He personally spent hours with union leaders and company managers trying to settle strikes.

But some railroad union leaders refused even to discuss settlement. Truman went before Congress to announce he was calling out the army to operate the trains. Tremendous amounts of coal and food had to be produced in the United States and shipped to Europe quickly, as the Europeans were starving and freezing to death in the coldest winter ever. While the president was telling Congress about what he intended to do, the railroad strike was settled.

In the meantime, the coal miners strike continued. President Truman ordered the government to take over operation of the coal mines in order to get the miners back to work while talks went on to reach a settlement. But still without a settlement, eight months later, the head of the coal miners' union called the workers out of the mines again. President Truman could not allow any union to strike against the U.S. government. He ordered the Justice Department to get court orders to make the coal miners return to work. The coal miners ignored the court orders. But when the union was fined $3.5 million for disobeying the laws of the United States, the strike ended.

The strikes made the American people angry. Congress passed a strong law to control strikes. It could delay strikes for an eighty-day cooling-off period. It forbade government workers to strike at all. It made industrywide strikes and sympathy strikes by other unions illegal. It would not allow unlawful strikers to get their jobs back. It forbade all union worker shops, and union leaders had to sign non-Communist oaths. President Truman thought the legislation was unfair to labor. He vetoed it, calling it a slave labor law. The Congress overrode his veto, and the Labor-Management Relations Act of 1947, known as Taft-Hartley, became law.

In his role as President, Truman kept a steady stream of ideas for legislation flowing from the White House up Pennsylvania Avenue to Congress. A very important law he asked Congress to pass was for the control of atomic energy. On October 3, 1945, he proposed an Atomic Energy Commission.

The Atomic Energy Commission would consist of five people appointed by the President and confirmed by the Senate to direct and control everything related to atomic energy. But Truman reserved the right of the President alone to decide when and where an atomic weapon could be made, tested, or used. After the atomic bomb was exploded over Hiroshima, Truman realized that it had the power to destroy the world. His science advisers also told him atomic energy could be harnessed to help the world. It was a powerful but unknown resource that needed more research. The U.S. government had spent $2.5 billion to pay the best scientists and to build laboratories and factories for them to work in. President Truman wanted to keep those research teams active, producing better weapons for defense and finding peaceful uses for atomic power.

A fire storm broke out in Congress over his Atomic Energy Commission proposal. The army and navy opposed it and pushed for their control of the atomic bomb since it was a weapon. President Truman felt civilian control of atomic energy was necessary to turn atomic knowledge to peaceful uses. This was an American tradition, just as the commander-in-chief of the armed forces had always been a ci-vilian President. Some high government officials wanted to share atomic secrets freely with the rest of the world. Truman was determined that the secret of how to make the bomb would remain within the United States. He finally persuaded Congress to see it his way. Atomic power has always re-mained under tight civilian government control.

Harry Truman had other plans for the army and navy. Since 1906, he had been a soldier working his way up in the Missouri National Guard and Army Reserve from private to colonel. Now he was commander-in-chief of all the armed services. Through his work in the Truman Committee when he was a senator, he had seen much waste in the military. For example, in many places the army and navy had camps and bases next to each other, but one service could not use the other's property, though it *all* belonged to the U.S. government. The navy had its own little army—the marines. In the cabinet, there was a secretary of war and a secretary of the navy. Soon a secretary of the newly created separate air force would be named. Often there was jealousy over which service would get the most dollars from Congress. Worst of all was the lack of communication between the army and navy that contributed to the staggering losses at Pearl Harbor.

President Truman wanted a more streamlined fighting force that would interact, be more efficient, and save money. The commander-in-chief knew a strong force had to be ready to stand up to the Russians anyplace in the world. Yet the 8 million people in the military services during the war were clamoring to return to civilian life. He had to make less do more. The only way was to unify the services under one head, a secretary of defense.

The same problem occurred in intelligence gathering. The State Department, the FBI, the OSS (Office of Strategic Services), the army, and the navy all gathered information from different parts of the world. The President got some but not all of this information. Truman persuaded Congress to create the CIA—the Central Intelligence Agency—where all communications would come into one place. After that, the President's first appointment every day was with the director of the CIA, who gave him the important information gathered in the past twenty-four hours.

The way the Soviet Union was acting, President Truman needed all the information he could get to make important decisions every day that would affect people all over the world. Greece had bravely resisted the Germans and Italians before being overrun. After the war, Greece was powerless, its people starving. The Russians applied pressure to establish a Communist government in Greece. But the Greek people voted for a return of their king. In the northern mountains, Communists poured in from neighboring Yugoslavia and began a civil war. They kidnapped thousands of Greek children and sent them to Communist countries to be trained. Britain sent in troops, but by 1947, the British could no longer afford to help the Greeks. President Truman knew that the United States alone had to stop the spread of communism from enslaving Greece and Turkey.

On March 12, 1947, he put forth a new foreign policy for the United States. It called for aid to help free people resisting takeovers by Communist minorities within their countries or by outside military forces. Not only did members of Congress of both parties support this program, but so did the free people of the world. It gave them hope. They called it the Truman Doctrine. The United States sent $400 million in aid to Greece and Turkey. In addition, United States advisers helped to rebuild railroads, canals, and factories there. The U.S. fleet made visits to Greek ports to warn the Communists to stay away. Greece and Turkey remain free countries today.

The Greeks were not the only people for whom Truman had great concern. No matter how much food was sent overseas, millions still did not have enough to eat. Britain could not help any longer since it was close to bankruptcy. The United States even had to make an emergency loan of $3.5 billion to Britain. The United States gave money to other countries, too. But these were stopgap measures, not a cure for Europe's desperate problems.

Harry Truman never forgot the suffering of his family after the Civil War. From their experiences, he was determined to help Europe rise from its ashes. He feared that without economic recovery in Europe so its countries could buy U.S. goods, the depression would return.

President Truman called in Secretary of State George C. Marshall to help him. They had an idea that was not just throwing more emergency aid at European countries, but a plan for Europeans to help themselves. An important feature of the plan was that the countries would have to invest their own money equal to the amount given by the American government. And they would have to work together. As a first step in the plan, sixteen countries met in Paris, France, and outlined their needs. Mr. Truman talked over radio to the American people and went before Congress to explain that the $17 billion he was requesting was to *rebuild* Europe within four years. It was an enlargement of the Truman Doctrine to stop communism by making European countries strong again.

After much wrangling in Congress, the European Recovery Act finally was passed in early 1948. Food, fuel, machinery, military aid, and technical advisers were sent to Europe until 1951. During that time, farm production jumped 11 percent above prewar levels. The Europeans could feed themselves again. Industrial production was up 40 percent. Western European nations were on their way to undreamed of well-being. The program worked so well, only $13 billion in U.S. aid was needed. A British government official called it "a lifeline to sinking men."

This generous act proved to be one of the most successful foreign policies of the United States. Mr. Truman insisted it be called the Marshall Plan for Secretary of State Marshall, who guided it to success. Marshall was awarded the Nobel peace prize for his work, the only former military man to receive this honor.

The Russians were infuriated by the passage of the Marshall Plan because they would no longer be able to put Communist governments into helpless European countries. Stalin acted quickly by cutting off all trade between Communist countries in Eastern Europe with those countries in Western Europe. As Winston Churchill warned in a speech at Westminster College in Fulton, Missouri, back in March 1946, "an iron curtain has descended across the continent [of Europe]. . . ."

By the Truman Doctrine and the Marshall Plan, the United States and its democratic allies, known as the Free World, tried to *contain,* or stop, the spread of communism. This titanic and constant struggle of communism versus democracy all over the world became known as the *cold war.* The weapons were many: the ideas of democracy versus communism to capture the minds of people; economic power

Winston Churchill after delivering his famous "Iron Curtain" speech in Fulton, Missouri, in 1946. President Truman is standing behind him.

to aid weak countries; guerrilla warfare to undermine governments. Each side built more and more powerful weapons, especially atomic missiles.

Then Stalin brought the world to the brink of war by trying to force the United States, France, and Britain out of Berlin. The city of Berlin lay in the Soviet-occupied zone of eastern Germany. The Soviet Union sealed off all access between western Germany occupied by American, British, and French armies and Berlin. In Berlin itself, each country controlled an area like a pie divided into four pieces. The

United States had made an oral agreement with the Russians in the closing days of the war that assured free access to Berlin from the western part of Germany. But in 1948 the Russians broke the agreement by blocking the use of the railroads, canals, rivers, and highways. The only way to get in and out of Berlin was by air. Without supplies, 2 million Berliners in the U.S.–, British–, and French-occupied sectors would starve. Many plans were suggested to Truman to meet this dangerous crisis: force an armored train through, drop an atomic bomb on Moscow, get all American troops out of Europe and leave it to the Soviet Union.

Truman rejected these ideas. On June 26, 1948, he decided to supply Berlin by air. There was a *written* agreement with the Soviet Union to allow flights over the Soviet-controlled sector of Germany. Truman knew he was risking war, but he was determined to have the United States and its allies stay in Berlin no matter what the Soviet Union did. The United States appealed to the United Nations. But the Soviet Union vetoed every action the UN wanted to take. Meanwhile, U.S. and British planes flew clothing, food, and fuel into Berlin until May 12, 1949, when the Soviet Union ended the blockade.

The Berlin Blockade caused the United States to change its longstanding policies about entering into peacetime military alliances. On April 4, 1949, the United States and eleven other countries signed the North Atlantic Treaty setting up the North Atlantic Treaty Organization they called NATO. The member nations pledged to aid each other and West Germany if attacked. A strong and united Europe backed up by Canada and the United States, they hoped, would discourage further Soviet aggression and prevent a major war. Since NATO was set up for common

The Berlin Airlift, 1948. These children watch as an American plane bringing food and supplies flies overhead.

defense, President Truman insisted it be another self-help program. That is, each nation member should pay a share of the cost and provide troops and equipment.

Harry Truman was determined to prevent the spread of communism into the Western Hemisphere. He wanted to strengthen friendship among the countries of North and South America. In 1947 he visited Mexico and Canada. In Brazil, he signed for the United States along with leaders of twenty other Western Hemisphere nations the Inter-american Unity Treaty. The twenty-one countries agreed never to fight one another and to defend jointly any Western Hemisphere country that might be attacked.

The Truman family sailed home from Brazil aboard the battleship *Missouri*. This was their only semivacation together during Harry Truman's first term as President. Mrs. Truman and their daughter spent every summer in Independence. The President, too, felt a strong need to be with Missourians. He could depend on them to tell him whether they thought he was doing right—or wrong. They were not afraid to speak up to old Harry. But his visits usually turned into almost friendly riots. Large crowds gathered everywhere he went. They watched him get a haircut from an old Battery D buddy. Many people stood in front of the Truman home night and day.

In 1946, Harry and his brother, Vivian, managed to buy back the house and part of Blue Ridge Farm at Grandview so their mother could go home again. Early the next year, she broke her hip. This time it did not heal. Harry Truman flew frequently from Washington, D.C., to Grandview to be with her, conducting the presidency from the Muehlebach Hotel in Kansas City. On July 26, 1947, Martha Young Truman died. Harry Truman missed his mother deeply. Whenever he was away from Missouri, they had written letters to each other almost every day. Now his best friend, his mother, rested beside his father. These two people had given him the moral character, the courage, and the sense of right from wrong he needed to be President of the United States.

☆ *Chapter 10* ☆

"Give 'Em Hell, Harry!"

Martha Truman had once said she would wave a flag if her son were elected President in his own right. She did not live to wave that flag. But before she died, only she urged him to run for President in 1948. No one else did.

Almost from the time Harry Truman was cast into the presidency he did not seek, he was constantly criticized. Labor was against him because he had seized the coal mines and almost seized the railroads. Labor forgot that he had vetoed the Taft-Hartley bill. He was loudly condemned for having a balcony built off the second story of the White House. After it was built at a cost of fifteen thousand dollars, everyone had to admit it improved the look of the place. He trusted old friends who betrayed his trust, and Truman was blamed for their misdoings. The sport shirts he wore on vacation in Key West were viewed as too loud. He was referred to as a "little man," though he was only two or three inches less than six feet. He was even judged too cheerful most of the time. The people, the press, the Democratic party itself could not forgive him for not being Franklin Roosevelt.

Harry Truman never tried to be anyone but himself. He was determined not to get a case of what he called "Potomac

Fever," that is, thinking he was anybody so superimportant he could do anything he wanted to do. When the bands played "Hail to the Chief," Harry Truman knew it was for the office of the President of the United States, not for Harry Truman, the man.

His popularity rating of 70 percent in the polls in 1945 fell to only 36 percent in early 1948. But President Truman said, "A man who is influenced by the polls or is afraid to make decisions which may make him unpopular is not a man to represent the welfare of the country. . . . A President cannot always be popular. He has to be able to say *yes* and *no.*" He kept a saying on his desk by another Missourian, Mark Twain—"Always do right: this will gratify some of the people and astonish the rest."

Harry Truman thought one of the reasons for his unpopularity was that the American people were being misled by the press. The people did not know the true story of what he was doing in domestic and foreign affairs. He decided to tell them personally. In June 1948 he set out from Washington, D.C., and traveled to California, making a total of seventy-six speeches, many from the back platform of his train. People liked what he had to say. When Truman saw the people were for him, he made the final decision to seek another term in office. He was sure he could be reelected.

But the leaders of the Democratic party were convinced that they would lose the 1948 presidential election if Truman was their candidate. They urged him not to run. They wanted to draft the popular General Dwight Eisenhower. But Eisenhower dashed their hopes when he told them he was not interested.

The delegates to the 1948 Democratic National Convention that hot July in steamy Philadelphia were a discouraged lot. Some Democrats had split off from the main party to form the Progressive party. They nominated former vice president Henry Wallace as their candidate. Thirty-five delegates from three southern states walked out of the convention and formed their own States' Rights party, nicknamed the Dixiecrats, with Governor Strom Thurmond of South Carolina as their candidate. Why? Because Harry Truman insisted the Democratic party come out strongly for civil rights. The Democratic party had always *said* it supported civil rights; Harry Truman *meant* it. "I knew that it might mean the difference between victory and defeat in November. I knew, too, that if I deserted the civil-liberties plank of the Democratic party platform I could heal the breach, but I have never traded principles for votes, and I did not intend to start the practice in 1948 regardless of how it might affect the election."

A year and a half before, President Truman had appointed a committee to investigate the status of civil rights in the United States. He took this action because of many anti-minority incidents that took place after the war. He was especially angered by harassment of returning black soldiers and sailors.

In addition, people were beginning to realize another great injustice had been done. In the throes of war hysteria after the attack on Pearl Harbor, President Franklin Roosevelt had signed executive order 9066. This order forced 41,000 Japanese and 71,500 nisei, or American-born Japanese, living in Pacific coast states to leave their homes and businesses on a few days' or even hours' notice. These Japanese and Japanese-Americans were sent to desolate relocation camps in several states. Many lived in poor conditions behind barbed wire until the end of the war in 1945. Although they had not been accused or convicted of any crime, men, women, and children had been denied their basic rights guaranteed under the Constitution. Truman remembered that his mother had been only eight years old when she was forced into an internment camp in Kansas City during the Civil War. He had seen what Hitler did to people in concentration camps just because they were Jews.

After he received the committee's report on civil rights, he went before Congress on February 2, 1948, and asked for strong legislation to insure the civil rights of all people living in the United States. His program called for a federal antilynching law and a strengthening of existing civil rights laws. He insisted on an end to segregation on interstate buses and trains and repeal of the Immigration Act of 1924, which included provisions forbidding Asians to immigrate to the United States.

When Congress failed to act on his civil rights proposals, President Truman issued executive orders in July 1948 establishing fair employment practices in federal government jobs and desegregating the armed services. The generals and especially the admirals strongly opposed him. His cabinet and the Joint Chiefs of Staff and Congress advised him against such a move. But Truman thought integration would strengthen the fighting forces. From his own experiences, there is no room for segregation when soldiers are under enemy fire.

Harry Truman went against his own southern heritage. His Grandfather Young had owned slaves, and his family were Confederate sympathizers. But when anyone questioned his stand on civil rights, he often read them the Bill of Rights. Just as in his seemingly hopeless campaign for reelection to the Senate in 1940, he had to *do right*, even if it meant he could lose an election.

At the Philadelphia convention, Senator Richard Russell of Georgia offered himself to the Democratic party as an alternative to President Truman. He got 263 delegate votes; Truman got 947. The Democrats were so sure of defeat in the November election that Truman at first could not find anyone willing to accept the nomination as vice president. Supreme Court Justice William O'Douglas turned down his offer. Senator Alben Barkley, minority leader of the Senate, asked President Truman if he might run for vice president. He was seventy years old, but Harry Truman said he would be glad to have him.

The President arrived in Philadelphia on the evening of July 14. He expected to make his acceptance speech before the convention at 10:00 P.M., prime radio time across the United States. But he was kept waiting until 2:00 A.M. before he was escorted to the podium to speak to the convention. The delegates were hot, exhausted, and all but asleep by this time; they were too tired to cheer. Besides, they knew old Harry was the most boring speaker on earth.

Harry Truman stood straight and wide awake as he peered out at the crowd. Hundreds of harsh lights reflected off his thick glasses. He waited until all was quiet. Suddenly he shouted, "Senator Barkley and I will win this election and make these Republicans like it—don't you forget that." He meant it. To the dispirited delegates, he sounded like a man who knew the Democratic party would win. The delegates jumped to their feet, cheering. They wanted to believe him. He reminded them what the Democratic party had achieved and what the Republican party had not. Then he played one of the most famous political maneuvers of all time. He announced he was going to call the Republican Eightieth Congress back into special session on July 26, Turnip Planting Day in Missouri. The country could see if they would or would not pass the programs that their candidate for President, Thomas E. Dewey, was promising the voters. The delegates went crazy over his fighting speech.

The special session of Congress lasted fifteen days. President Truman asked for legislation on the housing crisis, a slowing of inflation, increases in Social Security, a national health plan. Almost nothing was passed. From then on, Truman reminded the voters about the "Do Nothing Republicans" ten times a day for the next two months. The Republicans realized, too late, they had been tricked.

Harry Truman took his campaign to the people just as he had in Missouri in his bids to be a judge and a senator. But instead of driving his car into the rural counties and talking in country stores and from the steps of courthouses, he boarded a train. The train stopped at large cities and small towns. Local politicians would join the train at every stop. While a high school band played, Harry Truman would come out on the back platform of the train. He introduced Mrs. Truman and their daughter, Margaret. He tailored each speech to the concerns of the local people he was addressing. Just as Truman finished talking, the train would slowly pull out of that station as everyone on the back platform smiled, waved, and hoped they had changed some voters' minds.

Truman made speeches from dawn until midnight. He talked off the cuff, never using a prepared speech. People liked him to tell it in his own colorful language. His audiences admired his undaunted spirit in the face of certain defeat, as all the polls showed he was the underdog. One day in Seattle during a speech lambasting the Republicans,

President and Mrs. Truman with their daughter, Margaret, returning from a campaign train trip during the 1948 election. Harry Truman made 356 speeches during that campaign, many from the back of this train.

somebody in the crowd yelled, "Give 'em hell, Harry!" From then on, people yelled it everywhere he went.

The Republicans tried to belittle his speeches at small, unimportant towns as "whistle-stops." Truman took the term and used it. He said he loved "whistle-stopping" up, down, and across the country, and the word became part of the language.

The Truman train traveled 31,700 miles in 35 days. The President made 356 speeches averaging 10 speeches a day. At the end, he went home to Independence and spoke by radio to the nation from his living room. He said, "From the bottom of my heart I thank the people of the United States for their cordiality to me and for their interest in the affairs of this great nation and of the world. I trust the people because when they know the facts they do the right thing. I've tried to tell them the facts and explain the issues." Then it was up to the voters.

The next day, November 2, was election day. From the beginning Harry Truman was ahead in the vote count. But even when his margin was 2 million votes, newspapers refused to believe it. One printed large headlines saying "DEWEY DEFEATS TRUMAN." Harry Truman's victory was the biggest upset in American political history.

On the morning of his inauguration, he had breakfast with the members of Battery D. At first they called him "Mr. President" until Truman insisted they go back thirty years to "Captain Harry." They formed an honor guard and marched in two long lines beside the president's car. Coming into office this time, Truman rode in a colorful parade down Pennsylvania Avenue, not in a funeral procession for Roosevelt. He was surrounded by cheering crowds instead of crying ones. On January 20, 1949, at 12:29 P.M. on a huge red, white, and blue decorated platform in front of the Capitol, Harry S. Truman was sworn into office for a second time by his old friend, Chief Justice of the United States Fred Vinson.

President Truman's inauguration speech was memorable.

One of the most famous American election photos. Truman holds up the newspaper that inaccurately declares his defeat.

It contained four main points. But Point Four, as it became known, was a plan for a worldwide, continuing program to help less-developed nations help themselves to a better life. It was not a money giveaway. It was a spreading of U.S. technical knowledge and know-how. He said, "Our aim should be to help the free peoples of the world, through their own efforts, to produce more food, more clothing, more materials for housing, and more mechanical power to lighten their burden. . . . We invite other countries to pool their technological resources in this undertaking. . . . It must be a world-wide effort for the achievement of peace, plenty, and freedom."

This idea became the Act for International Development in 1950. Thirty-four million dollars were authorized to begin the work. Thousands of technicians were sent into many countries; Truman called them "technical missionaries." Hundreds of trainees from needy countries came to the United States for education. The program reduced disease and relieved famine by helping countries grow more of their own food. It set up hydroelectric power plants and banking systems. Point Four proved to be a strong remedy against the spread of communism. Truman thought it was the United States' greatest contribution to peace. This work continues today through the Peace Corps.

During his second term, the Trumans had to move out of the White House because it was falling down around them. In 1945, Mrs. Roosevelt had warned them the place was full of rats. The leg of Margaret Truman's piano broke through the floor one day. Huge chandeliers swayed and threatened to crash. At times floors felt as if they were floating when anyone walked across them, and indeed they were. Nothing was holding them up but history. Steel supports had to be put everywhere to hold up the ceilings. President Truman requested Congress to set up a commission on Renovations of the Executive Mansion. After detailed study, the commission recommended that the White House be torn down and another one built.

But the White House meant so much to the American people, President Truman insisted the architects try to find ways to save it. The outer sandstone walls seemed to be strong and were allowed to remain standing, but everything inside the building was gutted. Workers dug a new two-story basement and laid a concrete foundation. The heating system was replaced and air-conditioning installed. The number of rooms was increased from 125 to 132. The entire interior of the house was restored to look almost exactly

The White House underwent a complete renovation during
Truman's second term in office. The outside was left standing, but
the inside was completely rebuilt and seven more rooms were added.
This photo shows the controversial balcony Truman had built. The
men are members of the White House commission overseeing the
reconstruction.

the way it had been. The cost was $5,761,000. Meanwhile, the Trumans lived across Pennsylvania Avenue at the historic 120-year-old Blair-Lee House. They did not move back into the White House until March 27, 1952, and lived there less than a year.

The Secret Service, charged with guarding the President, did not want the Truman family to live in Blair House. It was too hard to guard because it was right on Pennsylvania Avenue, with people walking past on the sidewalk a few feet from the front door.

Their worst fears were realized on the afternoon of November 1, 1950. Oscar Collazo and Griselio Torresola of the Puerto Rican Nationalist movement for an independent Puerto Rico tried to shoot their way into Blair House and kill the President.

The day was warm and all the windows and doors of Blair House were open. The time was 2:20 P.M. The two men approached from opposite directions. Torresola stopped at a guard booth and started a conversation with the White House police officer, Leslie Coffelt, to distract him. Meanwhile, Collazo walked to within eight feet of Donald Birdzell, another White House police officer, who was standing on the first step leading up to the open front door of Blair House. Collazo pulled out his gun and fired at Birdzell, wounding his leg. Birdzell ran out into Pennsylvania Avenue and Collazo started to run up the ten steps to Blair House. Another guard and a Secret Service agent shot at Collazo. Torresola shot Leslie Coffelt three times and then pumped three more shots into another police officer. He shot down Birdzell in the middle of the street. Coffelt managed to get off a shot and killed Torresola. Several other Secret Service men now on the scene shot down Collazo, although they

The Trumans lived at Blair-Lee House (right) while the White House was being rebuilt. The assassination attempt on President Truman and the shoot-out that followed took place in front of this building on November 1, 1950.

did not kill him. Twenty-seven shots were fired in three minutes.

Upstairs in his bedroom facing the street, President Truman heard the noise and put his head out the window. The guards urged him to get back. Inside, Secret Service men stood ready with submachine guns. They did not know if this might be an all-out assassination attempt of which the two men already shot were only the beginning.

It was ironic for two Puerto Ricans to attempt to assassinate President Truman. He had persuaded Congress to pass laws permitting Puerto Ricans to elect their own governor and control their own affairs, although the island remained a United States possession.

After the shooting was over, the President and Mrs. Truman insisted on going to a ceremony at Arlington National Cemetery as scheduled. As when his life was threatened in the Senate, he figured if he had survived World War I, he was not going to worry.

But the Trumans had to live under tight security until they moved back to the White House a year and a half later. They came and went by way of a back door in the alley behind Blair House. In front of the house, no one was allowed to walk on the sidewalk anymore.

Five days after the assassination attempt, Press Secretary Charlie Ross died. On December 5, 1950, while preparing to give an interview, Ross suddenly slumped over his desk at the White House. Harry and Bess Truman were deeply saddened for Charlie Ross had been their schoolmate through elementary and high school. He had gone on to become a distinguished professor at the University of Missouri, an editor of the *St. Louis Post Dispatch* newspaper, and a Pulitzer prize–winning journalist. But Charles Ross will best be remembered as press secretary and good friend to President Harry Truman during five historic years.

Later that same evening, Margaret Truman, who had pursued a successful career as a classical singer since graduating from college, was scheduled to give a concert at Constitution Hall in Washington, D.C. The next day a Washington newspaper music critic printed a very unflattering review of Margaret Truman's performance. Harry Truman, as her father, fired off a scathing letter to the critic defending his daughter in very colorful language. The President's letter was printed on the front page of most newspapers in the country. President Truman's White House advisers were panic stricken. But a lot of people thought he did the right thing as a parent. Truman never doubted it.

☆ *Chapter 11* ☆

The Commander-in-Chief

Shocking news changed the balance of power in the world the summer of 1949. On September 2, a U.S. Air Force plane studying weather conditions over the northern Pacific Ocean found high levels of radioactive material in the air. After scientists analyzed this information, they told the president that the Soviet Union must have exploded an atomic bomb somewhere in northern Asia. President Truman and his advisers were taken by surprise. They had estimated this would not happen until 1952, but they knew it would happen.

Shortly after becoming president in 1945, Truman had been given proof of spying among people in high government positions. By 1947 he had established a loyalty program among government workers. He and the Congress started investigations revealing incidents of espionage. These led to the Whittaker Chambers–Alger Hiss case, which a young congressman named Richard Nixon worked on. In 1950 the government made public the existence of a British-American spy ring. This led in 1953 to the execution of the Rosenbergs for passing atomic secrets. The Communist take-over of mainland China in 1949 and the explosion of an atomic bomb by the Soviet Union also in 1949 heightened fears of subversion, especially in the United States State Department.

Beginning in 1950, the accusations by Senator Joseph R. McCarthy of Wisconsin pushed many Americans beyond fear into hysteria. McCarthy had charged that the Communists were working in the government. Innocent people began to be accused of being Communists or Communist sympathizers. When even Truman's friend, General George C. Marshall, was attacked by the forces of Senator McCarthy in 1951, the president tried to stop the tidal wave of panic flooding the country. He knew such incidents had happened before in American history, starting with the Salem Witch Trials in 1692. Each time the American people had almost given up some of their precious freedom. This was the greatest danger.

Meanwhile, the Soviet Union was made bold by possession of an atomic bomb. After the defeat of Japan, there were not enough American troops to accept the surrender of the Japanese army in Korea. The Soviet Union agreed to handle the surrender north of the 38th parallel of the earth's latitude and the Americans took control south of it. Korea had been occupied by the Japanese since 1895. U.S. and Soviet troops were to be there only long enough to get the Japanese out. But the Soviet Union defaulted on its Potsdam agreement and turned northern Korea into another Communist puppet state. This North Korean government called itself the Korean People's Republic. President Truman tried to reach a settlement with Stalin to unify the country, but Stalin refused. Truman went ahead and created the Republic of Korea in the American-occupied southern half of the country. The people held free elections, and U.S. troops pulled out when the South Korean government was firmly in charge. United States advisers trained and equipped a 65,000-man South Korean army. On Saturday, June 24, 1950, Korean People's Republic troops from the north of Korea armed with Soviet-built tanks invaded the Republic of Korea.

Harry Truman had gone home to Independence to spend a quiet four-day weekend when he received a call from Secretary of State Dean Acheson telling him about the invasion of the Republic of Korea. The President wanted to fly to Washington at once, but Acheson advised him not to risk a night flight that would alarm the country.

Mr. Acheson arranged an emergency meeting of the United Nations Security Council for Sunday afternoon. The Security Council passed a resolution denouncing the invasion. The Korean People's Republic was not a member of the United Nations. The resolution passed only because the Soviet delegate was not there to veto it. He had walked out of the Security Council in January over a different dispute.

President Truman flew back to Washington Sunday afternoon and held a meeting with his advisers at Blair House that evening. They decided on three immediate actions. All Americans had to leave Korea at once. General Douglas MacArthur, stationed in Japan, was ordered to send supplies to the South Korean army. The United States fleet in the Pacific Ocean moved toward Korea.

By Monday, the North Koreans had captured Seoul, capital of the Republic of Korea. The South Korean army was in full retreat. General MacArthur went to Korea to study the situation. He called for the use of U.S. troops. The president of the Republic of Korea begged for help.

On Tuesday the UN Security Council passed a resolution

ordering an immediate case-fire and a withdrawal of North Korean troops. It also called for member nations of the UN to give assistance to the South Koreans "to restore international peace and security in the world."

Harry Truman faced what he called the most difficult decision of his presidency because it involved the whole world. Should the United States go to war over a piece of territory that had little value to its security? Yet, what if the United States did nothing? The Communists would know they could invade other countries without fear of American reprisal. The United Nations, which had called for action by member nations, would probably collapse. President Truman had to move quickly. It was like the Berlin crisis in 1948. Again, he realized he was looking the strong possibility of World War III squarely in the face. He was determined not to let it happen.

On June 30, he ordered U.S. troops from Japan sent to the city of Pusan on the southern tip of Korea, the only place the North Koreans had not overrun. But they went under the United Nations flag. Britain also sent ships to help in this United Nations effort. Truman ordered General MacArthur to restrict the fighting to south of the 38th parallel. He hoped this limited defense of South Korea, later termed a "police action," would prevent a major war because the United States no longer had its eight-million-man war machine. The people and Congress had insisted on quickly disbanding much of the military service after World War II, though Harry Truman had warned against it. The troops he sent to Pusan were recent draftees with no battle experience. Yet these 10,000 U.S. troops with 25,000 South Koreans held off a ring of 90,000 North Koreans surrounding Pusan for two-and-a-half months. Never before had a U.S.

President ordered so many American troops into military action without Congress's voting for an official declaration of war. Yet Congress supported his actions.

By September 15, General MacArthur, who had been named Supreme Commander of the United Nations, gathered enough forces for a surprise invasion behind enemy lines at a place called Inchon near Seoul. This invasion cut the North Koreans' supply lines. U.S. troops at Pusan drove north and linked up with the UN Inchon invasion forces. By September 29, Seoul had been freed.

President Truman allowed MacArthur to cross the 38th parallel in pursuit of the North Korean army. But MacArthur was also instructed he must stop at the North Korean border with China at the Yalu River. Truman was greatly concerned that the huge army of Communist China might come into the war. In 1949, after a civil war, the Chinese Communists had taken control of China, in area the third largest country in the world, with its population of almost half a billion people. The Nationalist government of China, which had been an ally of the United States, France, and Britain against Japan during World War II, had to flee to the island of Formosa off the China mainland. Later Formosa became known as Taiwan. Both the Nationalist government and the Communist government claimed the legal right to rule all of China. Nationalist China was a member of the United Nation's Security Council; Communist China was not a member of the UN at all.

President Truman decided to meet with General MacArthur to discuss the war. MacArthur had not been in the United States since 1937, and Truman did not know him. In addition, Truman had indications that MacArthur did not agree with his plan of action about the conduct of the war. At dawn on Sunday, October 15, 1950, both men landed at Wake Island in the Pacific Ocean. MacArthur was optimistic about the war, predicting it would be over by the end of November. He even talked about the need for aid to all Korea and the supervision of free elections. President Truman asked him about the chances that Chinese troops or even Soviet troops might enter the war. MacArthur assured him there was little possibility of that happening with the coming of winter.

But only a few days after Truman and MacArthur met on Wake Island, Communist Chinese troops began to cross the Yalu River to join the North Koreans. When he returned to his command headquarters in Japan, MacArthur gave orders for the bridges on the Yalu River to be bombed. President Truman found out about these orders and canceled the bombing an hour before the planes were to take off. Truman allowed MacArthur to destroy only the North Korean side of the bridges. General MacArthur wanted to bomb bases in northern China that were supplying enemy troops in North Korea. The President said no because he and his advisers thought it would bring about a bigger war. The Soviet Union had warned that if the United Nations forces bombed China, the Soviet Union would strike back. Yet wave after wave of Chinese Communist troops came into the fighting. By January 10, 1951, they had recaptured Seoul.

MacArthur let it be known through newspaper interviews that he felt if he had been allowed to bomb northern China, this defeat would never have happened. Indeed, the war would have been won by now. From the beginning of the Korean War, General MacArthur had wanted to help the Nationalist Chinese on Taiwan invade the China mainland.

On October 15, 1950, President Harry S. Truman and General Douglas MacArthur met at Wake Island in the Pacific Ocean to discuss the Korean War.

Publicly, President Truman praised MacArthur as a brilliant general. Privately, he ordered him to stop giving interviews that publicly contradicted the President's policies or plans of action.

General Matthew Ridgeway was appointed UN commander in Korea when General Walton Walker was killed. Under General Ridgeway, the UN forces started a new offensive and by March 1951 were north of the 38th parallel again. President Truman thought this would be a good time to put forth a proposal for an armistice. He spent many hours with his advisers writing a carefully worded statement.

He secured the approval of other governments whose troops were fighting under the UN flag in Korea. But his message of peace was never sent. On March 24, 1951, General MacArthur issued his own statement demanding the Chinese Communists surrender. This was so contrary to President Truman's plan, he could not send his message for a cease-fire. The other countries who had just approved his proposed armistice clamored to know why this sudden change in U.S. policy. The war went on.

A few days later, General MacArthur sent a letter to a congressman, which was read to the House of Representatives. The letter openly criticized President Truman's foreign policy. MacArthur believed Communist China should be totally defeated. But Truman wanted a small police action war to prevent another world war in which atomic bombs might destroy the earth.

President Truman thought General MacArthur was insubordinate. He relieved MacArthur of his duties and replaced him as Supreme Commander of the United Nations with General Ridgeway. Harry Truman believed he had to take this action to carry out his oath as president to support and defend the Constitution.

The Constitution provides that policy be made by elected representatives of the people. The Constitution also says a duty of the president is to be commander-in-chief of the military. This was written into the Constitution in 1787 to prevent military officers from ever taking over the government as they had in many countries throughout history. President Truman interpreted this to mean that if he allowed any general to dictate policy, he would be handing the government over to the military. MacArthur had disobeyed direct orders from the commander-in-chief and thereby defied the Constitution.

Truman knew there would be a great outcry over the firing of MacArthur. He was right. Polls showed only 29 percent of the American people backed his decision. They were in a fury. Harry Truman was hanged in effigy. Some members of Congress talked about impeaching him. The President finally had to go on television and radio to explain his actions. He likened his firing of General MacArthur to President Lincoln's firing of General George McClellan during the Civil War.

Douglas MacArthur was a great hero who had served his country since 1903. He had been wounded three times and received the Medal of Honor. He had been a general in the Battle of the Argonne in World War I when Harry Truman was a captain. Despite being fired, General MacArthur returned to the United States in triumph, idolized by millions of adoring, cheering Americans. He was invited to make a speech before a joint session of Congress. Cities bestowed gifts on him as their way of showing appreciation for his long service to his country and strong disapproval of what President Truman had done.

Meanwhile, UN troops held their positions. On June 1, 1951, the secretary general of the United Nations suggested a cease-fire along the 38th parallel. A few weeks later, the Soviet government said peace discussions should begin. A first meeting between North Korean–Chinese and UN representatives was held July 10, 1952, at Kaesong near the 38th parallel. But there was no cease-fire. The talks dragged on until October 8, 1952, when they were broken off over prisoner exchange. President Truman knew many of the

132,000 Chinese and North Korean prisoners did not want to return home. He would not force them back into slavery. Fighting continued for the rest of Truman's presidency. The Korean War finally ended in July 1953. A total of forty-two nations participated in the war under the United Nations' flag. The UN became a force for maintaining world peace.

During the last year of Truman's presidency, a constitutional crisis occurred that threatened the outcome of the Korean War. It even threatened the United States' standing in the world in its struggle against communism.

American steelworkers sought higher wages, but the steel companies refused to bargain with them unless the companies were allowed to almost double the price of steel. President Truman saw this as an outright example of price gouging, which could upset the economy. When negotiations between the steel workers' unions, the steel companies, and the government failed, Truman issued executive order 10340 on April 7, 1952. This ordered the government to temporarily seize the steel mills as a last resort. He went on radio that evening to explain his action to the American people. "With American troops facing the enemy on the field of battle, I would not be living up to my oath of office if I failed to do whatever is required to provide them with the weapons they need for their survival."

But when the President asked Congress for legislation to operate the steel mills so supplies could continue to flow to the troops in Korea, Congress refused to act. What is more, on June 2, the Supreme Court ruled the seizure was unconstitutional. The strike did not end until July 24 when the steel companies were granted most of the price increases they had demanded.

☆ *Chapter 12* ☆

Welcome Home

When he was elected in 1948, Harry Truman decided he would not run for reelection in 1952. To his way of thinking, George Washington had set a wise precedent when he retired after two terms. Truman had publicly disapproved of Franklin Roosevelt's seeking a third term in 1940. But he supported him as a loyal Democrat when the party nominated Roosevelt again. In 1947 the Eightieth Congress had proposed the Twenty-second Amendment to the Constitution and two-thirds of the states passed it by 1951. This addition to the Constitution barred any President from serving more than two terms in office. However, the Twenty-second Amendment did *not* apply to Mr. Truman, since he was President when it was enacted. Still, he knew he would not use this privilege.

President Truman began searching for the person to be his successor. He wanted his old friend Chief Justice of the United States Fred Vinson to run for President. Vinson had been a congressman and an assistant to both Roosevelt and Truman. The chief justice thought the idea over for many months and then declined to be a candidate.

President Truman next looked to Governor Adlai Stevenson of Illinois. He came from a family of important

Democratic politicians, and he had served in the federal government. The President thought he was a good governor of Illinois, but Stevenson could not decide whether or not to be a candidate. Meanwhile, White House aides encouraged Truman to run again. Reluctantly, he thought he might have to, especially when General Dwight Eisenhower announced he was a Republican candidate. Truman was surprised at this turn of events because Eisenhower had always told him he was not interested in running for office.

Shortly before the 1952 Democratic Party National Convention, Governor Stevenson agreed to run. Truman saw to it that he was nominated. But almost immediately, Stevenson seemed to want to distance himself from the President. He moved his campaign headquarters out of Washington, D.C., to Springfield, the capital of Illinois. He talked about cleaning up the mess in Washington because the Republicans were accusing the Truman administration of being soft on communism and of corruption. This angered Harry Truman. He thought Stevenson should be running on the Democratic President's good record over the last eight years. The U.S. economy was booming and unemployment was low. Even more important, Harry Truman not only had saved a large part of the world from having communism forced on it, but the United States from communism and worse.

Shortly after becoming President in 1945, Truman had been given proof of spying for the Soviet Union among people in high government positions. By 1947 he had established a loyalty program among government workers. He and the Congress started investigations revealing incidents of espionage. These led to the Whittaker Chambers–Alger Hiss case, which a young congressman named Richard

Nixon worked on. In 1950 the government made public the existence of a British-American spy ring. This led in 1953 to the executions of Julius and Ethel Rosenberg for passing atomic secrets. The Communist take-over of mainland China in 1949 and the explosion of an atomic bomb by the Soviet Union also in 1949 heightened fears of subversion, especially in the United States State Department.

Beginning in 1950, the accusations by Senator Joseph R. McCarthy of Wisconsin pushed many Americans beyond fear into hysteria. McCarthy had charged that Communists were working in the government. Innocent people began to be accused of being Communists or Communist sympathizers. When even Truman's friend, General George C. Marshall, was attacked by the forces of Senator McCarthy in 1951, the President tried to stop the tidal wave of panic flooding the country. He knew such incidents had happened before in American history, starting with the Salem Witch Trials in 1692. Each time the American people had almost given up some of their precious freedom. This was the greatest danger.

But people were tired of the Korean War that dragged on. When Eisenhower promised he would go to Korea personally, the American people elected him by 6 million votes over Stevenson. Although Truman greatly admired General Eisenhower and had made him one of his chief advisers, the President resented the Republican candidate's turning the Korean War into a political football. President Truman felt that the United States must always present to the world a single foreign policy on which both Republicans and Democrats agree.

Yet once the election was over, Harry Truman was determined that the new President would know more about foreign and domestic affairs than he had when Franklin Roosevelt died. In his telegram of congratulations to Eisenhower on winning the election, he immediately proposed to cooperate fully in the transfer of government. He even offered Mr. Eisenhower the presidential plane, the *Independence,* to go to Korea, although he strongly disapproved of his going.

But the tough 1952 campaign left hard feelings between Truman and Eisenhower. The Eisenhowers refused the Trumans' invitation to the traditional preinaugural lunch at the White House. Eisenhower even refused to come into the White House to escort the retiring President out to the car they would ride in to the inaugural ceremonies at the Capitol. The old and the new presidents rode up Pennsylvania Avenue amid cheering crowds in silence as cold as the weather. Yet Harry Truman meant well when he ordered Major John Eisenhower home from Korea so he could be present when his father was sworn in as President. Eisenhower made a kind gesture when he lent the presidential railroad car to the Trumans to ride in comfort back to Missouri.

The transfer of actual power from one President to another took about one minute. The Truman presidency ended at noon, January 20, 1953. As soon as Dwight D. Eisenhower repeated the thirty-five words of the presidential oath, all the work and worry of the world's most powerful office descended on his shoulders. A free man at last, plain Mr. Truman walked over and shook hands with the only other living ex-president, his good friend Herbert Hoover. Then the Truman family quietly slipped away unnoticed while all eyes were on the new President.

Late that afternoon, nine thousand people came to the

The Truman home at 219 North Delaware Avenue in
Independence. This fourteen-room Victorian house was built in 1867
by Bess Wallace Truman's grandfather, George Porterfield Gates,
who owned a large flour mill. After Harry and Bess Truman were
married, they called this house home for the rest of their lives. It
was the summer White House during Truman's presidency.

Washington, D.C., train station to say good-bye to the
Trumans. Amid kisses and handshakes, they sang "Auld
Lang Syne" and "For He's a Jolly Good Fellow." The next
evening when the train reached Independence, Mary Jane,
Vivian, along with ten thousand relatives, friends, neighbors, and Missourians from miles around were waiting to
welcome the Trumans home. Five thousand more people
surrounded their house on Delaware Avenue. Harry and

Bess Truman were overcome with happiness. This display of deep affection made thirty years of political hard knocks seem almost worth it.

Mr. Truman went back to mowing the grass sometimes, and Mrs. Truman tended to their large house. They were alone in the old house for the first time in their marriage. Bess Truman's mother, Margaret Wallace, had died in the White House in 1952 at the age of 90. Their daughter, Margaret, made her home in New York City where she pursued a career in music. Once again, Harry Truman was out of a job. The ex-president did not receive a pension. Although business offers with huge salaries poured in, he knew they were for an ex-president, not for Harry S. Truman, and he refused to sell the presidency. He also declined invitations to become the president of universities because he lacked a higher education.

But Harry Truman was not ready to retire, and he resented being called a senior citizen. Soon he was back at work six days a week and a few hours on Sundays. He had to organize 300 crates and almost 500 steel filing cabinets filled with 3.5 million documents from his ten years in the Senate and two terms as President. The first thing he intended to do was write the history of his life while the events of his presidency were fresh in his memory. He thought so many lies had been told about him that he wanted to leave an accurate report of what he had done and why he had done it. His two books, *Memoirs: Year of Decisions* and *Memoirs: Years of Trial and Hope*, were published in 1955 and 1956. However, after he paid his income taxes and his assistants on the project, he had little money left. He wrote a shorter book titled *Mr. Citizen*, published in 1960.

The second thing Truman wanted to do was build a library

must be an honorable man and he must be a good politician in order to become a statesman under our form of government. If you will study the history of our country you will find that our greatest presidents and congressional leaders have been the ones who have been vilified most by the current press. But history justifies the honorable politician when he works for the welfare of the country.

"I would risk my reputation and my fortune with a professional politician sooner than I would with the banker or the business man or the publisher of a daily paper! More young men and young women should fit themselves for politics and government.

Some hand-written notes on politics and politicians by Harry S. Truman.

and museum. The library would serve as a research center where writers and scholars would have access to those 3.5 million papers. The museum would display the mementos of his presidency so people could see them and understand those years. One room was to be an exact reproduction of the Oval Office as it was when he was President. While some funds were donated, Harry Truman himself raised from lecture fees $1 million of the $1.75 million for the original library building. He had planned to build the library on Blue Ridge Farm in Grandview, but the city of Independence donated a beautiful park as the site for the library. Truman

The Harry S. Truman Library in a parklike setting in Independence, Missouri. It contains a replica of President Truman's office. Visitors can hear a recording of his voice describe the room. There are many personal objects of Mr. Truman's as well as historic items from his presidency on display. The library houses his millions of private and public papers and books about the Truman era.

hired the architect and planned every detail of his library inside and out. The building was completed and dedication ceremonies held July 6, 1957. On that day, Harry Truman gave the library and everything in it to the American people by transferring ownership to the United States government. The library is managed by the National Archives and Records Service.

The year 1956 was an eventful one for the Trumans. They went to Europe. In April their daughter, Margaret, married Clifton Daniel in Independence, at the same church where Harry and Bess had married thirty-seven years before. This marriage gave the former President and first lady four grandsons over the years. Nineteen fifty-six was also an election

Truman sitting at the desk he used in the White House while he
was President.

year. Again Stevenson ran and again Harry Truman hit the
campaign trail. But Eisenhower won a second term.

In 1960, with Eisenhower leaving office after eight years,
Harry Truman looked for a Democratic party candidate for
President. Senator John Kennedy came to the Truman Library asking for the former President's backing, but Truman
did not give it to him. He thought Jack Kennedy was too
young to be President. But when Kennedy became the party
nominee, Truman supported him. After President Kennedy

President Lyndon B. Johnson signed the 1965 Medicare Bill at the Truman Library in Independence. Seated at the table are President Johnson and former President Truman. Standing behind them are first lady Lady Bird Johnson, Vice President Hubert Humphrey, and former first lady Bess Truman.

was in the White House, he invited the Truman family to visit on two different occasions. The Trumans actually were glad to see again the place they once referred to as "The Great White Jail."

After President Dwight Eisenhower retired, he came to Independence to seek Harry Truman's advice on how to set up a presidential library in his own hometown of Abilene, Kansas. Harry Truman welcomed him as the third member of the ex-president's club.

When Vice President Johnson became President after Kennedy's assassination, he often called and visited Harry Truman in Independence. Johnson had been a young congressman from Texas when Truman was a senator. In 1965, President Johnson signed the Medicare bill at the Truman Library. It set up a government-run health insurance program for older people and the disabled. It helped them pay their hospital and medical bills. Finally, this part of President Truman's Twenty-One-Point Program, which he had proposed in 1945, was signed into law. President Johnson sent Harry Truman as his personal representative to the funeral of King Paul of Greece. Harry Truman was much loved in that country for the American programs and policies that had prevented a Communist takeover in the late 1940s.

In 1969, President Richard Nixon visited. He brought a gift for the Truman Library—the grand piano Harry Truman used to play in the White House.

On his eightieth birthday, Truman was given the great honor of being invited to address the United States Senate again. He was so deeply affected by this honor, he found it difficult to speak.

After he left office, when Harry Truman thought something needed to be called to the attention of the American people, he spoke out on radio, on television, and in the newspapers. By establishing the library, lecturing at colleges and universities, talking to schoolchildren, and writing, he continued to work for his country the rest of his life.

Harry S. Truman always was proud to be from Missouri. And he was proud to have been a farmer and a soldier. Most of all he was proud to be a politician. To his way of thinking, "Politics is 'the science and art of government.' Under our Constitution the 'art of government' is the art of understanding and working for the interest of the people. . . . A politician is a man who is interested in good government. . . . History justifies the honorable politician when he works for the welfare of the country. . . . More young men and women should fit themselves for politics and government."

Chronology of Important Dates
in the Life of Harry S. Truman

1881 Parents of Harry Truman, John Truman and Martha Ellen Young, marry.

1884 Truman born in Lamar, Missouri, on May 8.

1889 Begins to wear glasses.

1890 Truman family moves to Independence, Missouri.

1892 Starts first grade at Noland School with brother, Vivian.

1896 Meets Bess Wallace.

1901 Graduates from high school with Bess Wallace.

1903 Truman family moves to Kansas City. Truman finds work at a bank.

1905 Joins the Missouri National Guard.

1906 Truman family moves back to Young farm in Grandview, Missouri.

1909 Grandmother Harriet Louisa Young dies.

1910 Meets Bess Wallace again.

1913 Becomes secretly engaged to Bess Wallace.

1914 John Truman dies, November 3.

1917 United States declares war on Germany, April 6. Truman reenlists in the Missouri National Guard, June 22.

1918 Made commanding officer of Battery D and takes part in

the Battle of the Argonne, September 26. Armistice declared; World War I ends, November 11.

1919 Marries Bess Wallace, June 28. Truman and Edward Jacobson open haberdashery store in Kansas City.

1922 Elected a judge of Jackson County, Missouri.

1924 Mary Margaret Truman born, February 17.

1926 Wins reelection as judge.

1929 Stock market crashes, Great Depression begins.

1930 Wins reelection to a third term as judge.

1932 Franklin D. Roosevelt elected President of the United States.

1934 Truman elected to the U.S. Senate.

1938 Sponsors bill in Congress to establish Civil Aeronautics Board.

1940 His Transportation Bill reforming the railroads passed by Congress. Wins reelection to Senate.

1941 Establishes the Committee to Investigate the National Defense Program, April. Japanese attack Pearl Harbor, Hawaii, December 7.

1944 Elected Vice President of the United States.

1945 President Roosevelt dies; Truman becomes President, April 12. V-E Day—the war in Europe ends, May 8. Truman meets Churchill and Stalin in Potsdam, Germany, July. Atomic bomb dropped on Hiroshima, Japan, August 6; Nagasaki, August 9. V-J Day—Japan signs surrender papers; World War II ends, Sept. 2. Truman introduces Twenty-One-Point Program, the Fair Deal, to Congress. United Nations established, October 24.

1946 Philippine Islands granted independence.

1947 Truman Doctrine puts forth a new foreign policy, March 12. Twenty-second Amendment proposed limiting

President to two terms, March 24. Martha Young Truman dies, July 26.

1948 Marshall Plan to help European recovery. The Berlin Airlift. Desegregation of armed services and fair employment in federal jobs. Truman reelected President, November 2.

1949 Truman outlines Point-Four program to help less-developed nations. United States and eleven other countries establish NATO, April 4. Renovation of White House begins. Soviet Union explodes atomic bomb, August.

1950 North Korea invades South Korea, June 24. Two Puerto Ricans try to assassinate Truman, November 1.

1951 Truman dismisses General Douglas MacArthur as Supreme Commander of UN forces.

1952 Dwight D. Eisenhower elected President.

1953 Korean War ends, July 27.

1957 The Harry S. Truman Libary completed.

1965 President Lyndon Johnson signs Medicare Bill at Truman Library.

1972 Truman dies on December 26.

Sources

Introduction

Truman, Harry S. *Memoirs: Years of Trial and Hope.* Garden City,
New York: Doubleday, 1956.

————. *The Autobiography of Harry S. Truman,* ed. Robert H.
Ferrell. Boulder, Colorado: Colorado Associated University
Presses, 1980.

Chapter 1

Truman, Margaret. *Harry S. Truman.* New York: Morrow, 1973.

Steinberg, Alfred. *The Man from Missouri.* New York: Putnam,
1962.

Truman, Harry S. *Autobiography of Harry S. Truman.*

————. *Memoirs: Year of Decisions.* Garden City, New York:
Doubleday, 1955.

Miller, Merle. *Plain Speaking: An Oral Biography of Harry S. Truman.* New York: Berkley, 1974.

"Independence." *World Book Encyclopedia.* 1969 ed.

Truman, Margaret. *Bess W. Truman.* New York: Macmillan,
1986.

Miller, Richard L. *Truman: The Rise to Power.* New York:
McGraw-Hill, 1986.

Personal Papers of Harry S. Truman. Harry S. Truman Library, Independence, Missouri.

Harry S. Truman Library Institute Newsletter. Vol. 12, no. 4. Independence, Missouri: 1984.

Chapter 2

Truman, Harry S. *Autobiography of Harry S. Truman.*

Miller, Merle. *Plain Speaking.*

Truman, Margaret. *Harry S. Truman.*

———. *Bess W. Truman.*

Truman, Harry S. *Memoirs: Year of Decisions.*

———. *Dear Bess: The Letters from Harry to Bess Truman, 1910–1959,* ed. Robert H. Ferrell. New York: Norton, 1983.

Personal Papers of Harry S. Truman. Harry S. Truman Library, Independence, Missouri.

Harry S. Truman Library Institute Newsletter. Vol. 12, no. 4. Independence, Missouri: 1984.

Chapter 3

Truman, Margaret. *Bess W. Truman.*

Truman, Harry S. *Autobiography of Harry S. Truman.*

Miller, Richard L. *Truman: The Rise to Power.*

Miller, Merle. *Plain Speaking.*

Harry S. Truman Library Institute Newsletter. Vol. 15, no. 4. Independence, Missouri: 1987.

Harry S. Truman Library Institute Newsletter. Vol. 15, no. 1. Independence, Missouri: 1987.

Harry S. Truman Library Institute Newsletter. Vol. 12, no. 4. Independence, Missouri: 1984.

Chapter 4

Truman, Margaret. *Bess W. Truman.*
———. *Harry S. Truman.*
Miller, Richard L. *Truman: The Rise to Power.*
Miller, Merle. *Plain Speaking.*

Chapter 5

Miller, Richard L. *Truman: The Rise to Power.*
Truman, Margaret. *Bess W. Truman.*
Truman, Harry S. *Autobiography of Harry S. Truman.*
Truman, Margaret. *Harry S. Truman.*
Truman, Harry S. *Memoirs: Year of Decisions.*
Harry S. Truman Library Institute Newsletter. Vol. 14, no. 1. Independence, Missouri, 1986.

Chapter 6

Miller, Richard L. *Truman: The Rise to Power.*
Truman, Harry S. *Dear Bess: Letters from Harry to Bess Truman.*
———. *Autobiography of Harry S. Truman.*
Truman, Margaret. *Harry S. Truman.*
———. *Bess W. Truman.*
Miller, Merle. *Plain Speaking.*
Truman, Harry S. *Memoirs: Year of Decisions.*
Harry S. Truman Library Institute Newsletter. Vol. 6, no. 4. Independence, Missouri: 1978.
Harry S. Truman Library Institute Newsletter. Vol. 8, no. 1. Independence, Missouri: 1980.
Harry S. Truman Library Institute Newsletter. Vol. 8, no. 3. Independence, Missouri: 1980.

Chapter 7

Truman, Margaret. *Bess W. Truman.*
————. *Harry S. Truman.*
Truman, Harry S. *Memoirs: Year of Decisions.*
————. *Autobiography of Harry S. Truman.*
Ferrell, Robert H. *Off the Record.* New York: Harper and Row, 1980.

Chapter 8

Truman, Harry S. *Memoirs: Years of Trial and Hope.*
Chicago Tribune. April 14 and 15, 1945.
New York Times. April 14 and 15, 1945.
Truman, Margaret. *Bess W. Truman.*
Miller, Merle. *Plain Speaking.*
Personal Papers of Harry S. Truman. Harry S. Truman Library, Independence, Missouri.
Truman, Margaret. *Harry S. Truman.*

Chapter 9

Truman, Harry S. *Memoirs: Years of Trial and Hope.*
Truman, Margaret. *Harry S. Truman.*
Truman, Harry S. *Memoirs: Year of Decisions.*
Truman, Margaret. *Bess W. Truman.*
Steinberg, Alfred. *Harry S. Truman.*
Miller, Merle. *Plain Speaking.*
Harry S. Truman Library Institute Newsletter. Vol. 15, no. 3. Independence, Missouri: 1987.

Chapter 10

Truman, Harry S. *Memoirs: Year of Decisions.*
Truman, Margaret. *Harry S. Truman.*

Truman, Harry S. *Memoirs: Years of Trial and Hope.*

Census of 1850. Harry S. Truman Library, Independence, Missouri.

O'Neill, Thomas P., with William Novak. *Man of the House: The Life and Political Memoirs of Speaker of the House Tip O'Neal.* New York: Random House, 1987.

Truman, Harry S. *The Autobiography of Harry S. Truman.*

The White House. Washington, D.C.: White House Historical Association, 1973.

Harry S. Truman Library Institute Newsletter. Vol. 7, no. 4. Independence, Missouri: 1979.

Truman, Margaret. *Bess W. Truman.*

New York Times, November 2, 1948.

Chapter 11

Truman, Margaret. *Harry S. Truman.*

Truman, Harry S. *Memoirs: Years of Trial and Hope.*

Miller, Merle. *Plain Speaking.*

"Korea." *World Book Encyclopedia,* 1969 ed.

Chapter 12

Truman, Margaret. *Harry S. Truman.*

Truman, Harry S. *Memoirs: Years of Trial and Hope.*

Truman, Margaret. *Bess W. Truman.*

Harry S. Truman Library Institute Newsletter. Vol. 5, no. 1. Independence, Missouri: 1977.

Truman, Harry S. *Mr. Citizen.* New York: Geis Associates, 1960; distributed by Random House.

Truman, Harry S. *Off the Record.*

Personal Papers of Harry S. Truman. Harry S. Truman Library, Independence, Missouri.

For Further Reading

Collins, David. *Harry S. Truman: The People's President.* Champaign, Illinois: Garrard, 1975.

Faber, Doris. *Harry Truman.* New York: Abelard Schuman, 1972.

Ferrell, Robert H. *Truman: A Centenary Remembrance.* New York: Viking, 1984.

Gies, Joseph. *Harry S. Truman: A Pictorial Biography.* New York: Doubleday, 1968.

Hargrove, Jim. *Harry S. Truman, Thirty-third President of the United States.* Chicago: Children's Press, 1987.

Hudson, Wilma. *Missouri Farm Boy.* Indianapolis, Indiana: Bobbs-Merrill, 1973.

Kelton, Nancy. *Harry Four Eyes.* Milwaukee, Wisconsin: Raintree, 1977.

Leavell, J. Perry, Jr. *Harry S. Truman.* New York: Chelsea House, 1988.

Milton, David. *Harry S. Truman, The Man Who Walked with Giants.* Independence, Missouri: Independence Press, 1980.

Thomson, David S. *A Pictorial Biography of Harry S. Truman.* New York: Grosset and Dunlop, 1973.

Index

About the Author

☆   ☆   ☆

Karin C. Farley was born, raised, and still lives in the Chicago area. She earned several degrees at the University of Illinois, and currently she teaches college students. She has researched the lives of several presidents of the United States, with particular attention to the experiences and character traits they had as children. One of her previous books, *Canal Boy,* is the story of James A. Garfield, twentieth president, who worked on the Ohio canals as a teenager in the 1840s.

☆

Northport - E. Northport Public Library
185 Larkfield Road
E. Northport, N. Y. 11731
261-2313